306.7 C521r   FV
CHERFAS
THE REDUNDANT MALE : IS SEX
IRRELEVANT IN THE MODERN
WORLD?   15.95

THE
REDUNDANT
MALE

THE
REDUNDANT
MALE

IS SEX

IRRELEVANT

IN THE

MODERN WORLD?

JEREMY CHERFAS

JOHN GRIBBIN

PANTHEON BOOKS, NEW YORK

All rights reserved under International and
Pan-American Copyright Conventions.
Published in the United States by Pantheon Books,
a division of Random House, Inc., New York,
and simultaneously in Canada by
Random House of Canada Limited, Toronto.
Originally published in Great
Britain by The Bodley
Head **Ltd,** London.

Library of Congress Cataloging in Publication Data

Cherfas, Jeremy.
The redundant male.

Includes bibliographical references and index.
1. Men—Sexual behavior.   2. Sex.
I. Gribbin, John R.   II. Title.
HQ28.C54   1985   306.7   84-42971
ISBN 0-394-53030-6
ISBN 0-394-74005-X (pbk.)

Manufactured in the United States of America

First American Edition

For those of our friends
who still have a use for us

Our thanks to all the scientists and thinkers on whose work we have built, especially Mary Gribbin, Paul Ridd, Mark Ridley and Donald Symons, who were kind enough to read portions in draft. Their comments were invaluable. We are also grateful to Silke Bernhard and the Dahlem Konferenzen for the opportunity to bring the book to a satisfactory conclusion. Mary Gribbin also spent long hours searching through libraries at our behest.

Most of all, we are indebted to Jean Frere who suggested that we write the book and is now only too well aware of the cost of reproduction.

JEREMY CHERFAS
JOHN GRIBBIN
October 1983

'Sex is one of the nine reasons for reincarnation . . .
The other eight are unimportant.'

HENRY MILLER
Big Sur and the Oranges of Hieronymus Bosch

CONTENTS

PROLOGUE

THE PROBLEM

Why do women bother to have sons?

That stark question may strike you as foolish in the extreme. Women have no choice over whether they bear sons or daughters, there is no question of 'bother'. True, of course, but we intend a different sort of 'why', and our question goes to the heart of two of the great enigmas of biology. The first is the puzzle of sex, while the second is the puzzle of gender. Sex is simply a method of reproduction. It is a process of reproduction that requires two individuals to co-operate in the production of a new individual. From the human viewpoint, sex and reproduction appear as one, but they are not. There is an alternative. In the living world as a whole there are probably far more individuals for whom sex is at best a very rare event. Reproduction for them involves not two but one, that one splitting into two. The trouble is that this asexual majority, multiplying away without benefit of sex, is an unseen one, composed largely of invisible bacteria, single-celled plants and the like. In the visible world, sex does seem to dominate.

Sexual reproduction can occur without benefit of different sexes, and it does in many organisms, where any two individuals can get together to make new individuals. But in our species, like most of those we can see, it takes two types of individual, two genders, to make a new one. But doesn't sex include gender? Not necessarily, and that makes the second part of the puzzle. Gender is the business of sex roles, different mating types of a species being specialised to play different parts. One type is generally nurturant, producing a few large sex cells that are well endowed with food resources to enable growth of the offspring, and often taking care of those offspring beyond simply producing the sex cells. That sex we call female, and the sex cells they produce are eggs. The other sex we call male. By and large males take little care of their offspring, and their role is limited to contributing genetic material to the egg. Again, from our perspective sex and gender seem inextricable, so much so that we use the same word to denote both aspects of the process of

(1)

reproduction. But just as there are species that multiply without sex, so too there are many that have sex but no sexes.

So we can refine and rephrase our question as two different queries. Why do human females reproduce sexually? And why are there two genders with distinct properties? We will try in this book to answer those questions from the point of view of Charles Darwin's theory of natural selection.

That theory is so widely misunderstood that we should spell it out at the start. Living things vary slightly one from another. They also reproduce, and like begets like; the variations are passed to the next generation. But the resources needed to grow and reproduce are limited, so there is competition for those resources. Any heritable variation, no matter how slight, that gives its possessor an advantage in the competition for resources will tend to spread through the population because individuals with that variation will outreproduce individuals without it. The result is that variations will accumulate, populations will change and life will evolve. It really is simple; hereditary variation, coupled with a struggle for survival, must result in natural selection. But it took a man like Darwin to see how fruitful these simple ideas are.

Darwin's achievement was enormous, for he gave us an insight both into the vast diversity of life and the common characteristics that hold the diversity together. Living things are diverse because any that can exploit a slightly different way of making a living will prosper. All ways of making a living are exploited, and it is the range of possible livings—possible ecological niches—that gives us the range of life on Earth. But each living species is descended with modifications from some other form of life, and the underlying basic plans that have come down through the ages provide the mortar that binds together the diversity of different species.

To take a famous example, Darwin discovered thirteen different species of finch during his travels around the Galapagos islands. Each species had a different shape and size of bill because each had evolved to exploit a different source of food. The warbler finch has a long slender beak that it uses to probe for insects, while the large ground finch has a huge crushing beak for dealing with tough seeds. But despite their differences, all Darwin's finches share some overall similarities—they are all finches—because they are descended with modifications from a common ancestor. Diversity in detail accompanies similarity in basics.

Different beaks give the different finches an advantage because they enable the birds to exploit foods that no other birds are using. We explain the differences by natural selection. The explanations we seek will always be ones that tell us how particular biological possessions might benefit their owners. As we shall see, a female who produces equal numbers of male and female offspring seems to waste half of her potential in sons. But sex and gender have proved successful. They must have been advantageous to our ancestors or our ancestors would not have survived to produce us. If opting to have sex halves the reproductive success of a female there must be, or have been, considerable, but less obvious, evolutionary benefits that outweigh this obvious disadvantage.

So what is it about sexual reproduction and the division of labour by gender that has allowed these two processes to flourish? To make the existence of the problem crystal clear, imagine a population of male and female animals happily reproducing by means of sex. (This begs the question of how sex, and with it gender, arose; we come back to this later.) Now imagine that a mutant female arises, that is, one who differs genetically from the bulk of the population. She can do without males and still have young. Her offspring will be females who, like their mother, can reproduce without the help of males by a process called parthenogenesis. (From the Greek for virgin birth.) Because she does not produce males, such a female would have twice as many daughters as the other females; and because only daughters put much effort into raising offspring the mutation would spread very rapidly indeed. Within a very few generations all the females will be asexual. There is the cost of sons, dramatically brought into the open: they halve a female's capacity to reproduce. In such a species males would have become redundant, unless the female can obtain some parental care from her mate. If her partner too invests in their joint offspring the cost of sex to the female will be much lower because a female on her own will not do nearly as well as one with a mate. For males to have a continuing role, sexual reproduction must more than offset the twofold advantage of asexual reproduction. Plainly it has succeeded, so far as our own species and most of the animal world are concerned, so what are the advantages that it confers?

To be perfectly honest, nobody knows. That is why sex is such an enigma. There are plenty of ideas, though. The great British biologist Sir Ronald A. Fisher said in the 1930s that sex was one of the few biological phenomena that was kept around by the process called group selection. Group selection is a form of natural selection in which it is not individuals who succeed in outbreeding their fellows, but whole breeding populations. Members of one group might not individually breed as well as members of another group in a direct competition, but despite this their group does better as a whole. According to Fisher, groups that had evolved sex, despite the short-term disadvantage of having to produce males, enjoyed the more than compensatory advantage of faster evolution. This is because as a result of mating a sexual species can bring rare favourable changes together into a single body. An asexual species cannot. Thus the asexual species is likely to succumb to some change in the environment because it does not have the variability and flexibility to cope with the change. A sexual species is better able to adapt to the change and so survives. Although asexual populations expand more quickly than sexual ones, in the long run the asexual populations are doomed by their inflexibility. The sexual species survive, and give rise to new species, while the asexual ones die out, and this is why most of the species around today use sex to reproduce. But the advantage of sex is a long-term one only, needing enough time for species to arise and go extinct; it conveys no short-term evolutionary benefits.

Plausible though this may seem, most biologists who have studied the problem are unwilling to accept Fisher's account. The reason is that group selection is a very unlikely form of evolution. It will work, in theory, if conditions are just right; in practice, out in the natural world, conditions are seldom just right for group selection and it is very rare indeed. Most often the benefits gained by an individual who cheats, who abandons the harmful mutation of the group, will provide such an advantage that the cheat's offspring will quickly swamp the group. Nevertheless, there is some sparse support for Fisher's version of things. Parthenogenetic species do seem to go extinct quickly, compared to closely related sexual ones. But there seems to be a great deal more to be said against it.

The most telling argument against the idea of sex being a group selected phenomenon is the so-called balance argument put forward by George C. Williams of the State University of New York at Stony Brook. Williams asks us to imagine a population that can reproduce either with or without sex. Plenty of these exist, from strawberries to greenfly. In such a population, it would surely be easy for a mutant strain that does without sex entirely to arise simply by omitting one of the two options available. Such a mutation would spread rapidly if it provided a short-term benefit, and the population which persists with both methods would be displaced. But sex continues, which leads Williams to conclude that it must have short-term benefits that more than outweigh the immediate costs of males. Just what those advantages are will occupy part of this book, but essentially Williams (like Fisher) says that sex is good because it allows genetic shuffling which enables the organism to cope with an unpredictable future. Unlike Fisher, Williams says that the advantage of flexibility accrues to the *individual*, not to the group.

Williams likens the game of life to a lottery. An individual wins when its offspring themselves survive to maturity and reproduce, passing on the parent's genes. Since the parent has done just that during its own life, it has a winning ticket in the lottery. It could simply pass on that winning number: many copies of its own genes. If the same winning number will come up again, that is a good idea and the offspring will also win. But if the winning combination changes from one round to the next they all will do badly.

By contrast, although the sexual parent has only fifty tickets in the lottery for every hundred held by the asexual parent, each of those tickets—each offspring—carries a different number, a different genetic combination. If the winning number will change from generation to generation, one of those new combinations might still hit the jackpot. The lottery is the lottery of life, the prize is offspring who will succeed and reproduce, and the winning number is a particular genetic combination. To know whether Williams is correct we have to know how quickly the winning number changes; if it is relatively slow, so that offspring who are identical to their parent do best, then asexual copying will be favoured, but if it changes more quickly, so that slightly different offspring stand a better chance, then sex will win. As we will see, the rules of the game are everywhere different. Sometimes sex pays, and sometimes it doesn't.

There remains the question of the sexes themselves. Why are there two distinct sexes, and (putting to one side the exceptions that will prove so illuminating when we come later to consider them) why is it generally so easy to describe an organism as either male or female? This is not nearly so thorny a problem as that of sexual reproduction, and we will describe the likely origins of gender in detail in Chapter Three. In essence, what has happened is that males developed solely as carriers of genetic information. They contribute genetic material to the egg cell, which will become a new individual, but they originally made no direct contribution of resources to help the egg develop. Females, of course, have not stood by idly and allowed themselves to be exploited in this way. They have fought back, demanding investment by the male before they allow him access to their gametes. The investment may seem trivial—protection from the harassment of other males, as in the harems of sea lions—or it may be the ultimate sacrifice. A praying mantis who eats her suitor is putting his body to good use to nourish her eggs. Despite these countermeasures, there remains an all-important distinction between the sexes. Females *could* reproduce parthenogenetically if the egg cells could be induced to develop on their own. But males can never do so. Their sex cells, or gametes, have no store of food to use in the first stage of development. Males, from the level of gametes upwards, are utterly dependent on females in order even to enter life's lottery, and at a fundamental level the egg cell can be regarded as a resource for which sperm cells compete. If, for whatever reason, sexual reproduction loses its evolutionary edge and an asexual mutation arises, it must always be the female that provides the basis of the new line and the male that falls by evolution's wayside. This applies to our own species as much as to any other. Men are at best parasites on women, and at worst totally redundant in the immediate evolutionary scheme.

The problems are thus set out. We want to know why women bother to have sons. They could have twice as many descendants if they abandoned men and had parthenogenetic daughters. The curious genetic mixing that is sex must confer powerful evolutionary advantages to overcome that primary handicap. Is it simply a question of increased variability, or are there other factors? What are they? Then again, even though sex may be an advantage, gender is a separate question. Fungi manage without sexes, so why do we have sons and daughters, each with very different approaches to the business of sex? In our search for answers, we need to look first at the mechanics; bear with us while we do so, for only when the mechanisms of sex are clear will we be able to see how your own behaviour today has been moulded by four thousand million years of evolution. The conclusion we are inevitably led to requires this secure foundation, for it is our contention that the human male may have outlived his usefulness and could, in evolutionary terms, be redundant. Why then, do men exist at all? Females have control over the reproductive process and surely ought to have been able to escape their dependence on males. There is a conflict between males and females; perhaps males won the most recent round of the battle.

WHAT IS SEX?

Growth and reproduction are what life is all about. Only living things can replicate themselves, producing offspring which are themselves capable of reproduction. Essentially, the business of life is to garner resources wherever it can and use those resources to make copies of itself, to reproduce; all the diversity and all the complexity of life serves that one goal of reproduction.

Think of reproduction, and you will almost certainly think of sex, of two organisms coming together to contribute to the next generation. This is because most of the species with which we are familiar do indeed reproduce sexually. But there is an entire world of mostly unseen organisms that can reproduce without sex, and even among quite complex animals and plants there are those that manage entirely without sex. For many of these asexual organisms, growth and reproduction are one and the same; they grow until they are too big to be easily managed and then simply divide. It is a fair bet that all life on Earth was, at first, asexual. While the whole question of the origin of life is a puzzle beyond the scope of this book, if we want to understand the origin of sexual reproduction we have to go back to a time when there was no sex, when all reproduction was simply a question of growth.

Our understanding of the world is affected, quite literally, by what we can see. That is why we regard sex as *the* method of reproduction and it is also why we divide the living world into plants and animals. The differences between plants, able to harness the energy of the Sun directly, and animals, dependent ultimately on those plants to supply them with energy in the form of food, seem enormous. But to the biologist, especially one used to looking at life through a microscope, the distinction between plants and animals is almost insignificant. Far more important is the division between so-called eukaryotes, represented by plants and animals but also fungi and single-celled creatures that are both plants and animals, and prokaryotes, essentially bacteria but including also the blue-green algae.[1]

The differences between the two exist at the level of individual cells. Eukaryote cells have a well-developed nucleus, a central part of the cell which contains the hereditary material, the DNA. (The name is from the Greek *eu*, true, and *karyon*, kernel, because the cell's nucleus is likened to the kernel of a nut.) The rest of the eukaryote cell includes several different types of structure, or organelle, each of which performs some definite task in the life of the cell. There are the sausage-shaped mitochondria, which provide the cell with energy; the chloroplasts of plants, which trap sunlight; and the stacked membranes of the exotically named Golgi apparatus, which prepare substances for transport out of the cell, to name but three.

Prokaryote cells have no nucleus; their DNA is dispersed through the whole cell, often attached to the inside of the cell wall. There are also practically no internal organelles in a prokaryote, just the ribosomes where proteins are made and perhaps a flagellum that works like an oar to row the cell through the liquid in which it lives. Particularly relevant to us, prokaryotes do not have proper sex (they do exchange genetic material, as we shall see, but it isn't like real sex) while eukaryotes do.

The very first living things on Earth were prokaryotes. The oldest known fossils are very like modern bacteria, and they are found in rocks that are about 3.8 thousand million years old. (The Earth itself is probably only a little older, 4.5 thousand million years.) For almost the next 3 thousand million years all the fossils are prokaryotes. Some eukaryotes appear at around 800 million years ago, but it is not until about 600 million years ago that we find fossils that are recognisably animals, or plants, or fungi. For 75 per cent of the history of life on Earth, prokaryotes *were* life on Earth. So to discover where the eukaryotes, and with them sex, came from, we have to start with the prokaryotes.

For all their differences, prokaryotes and eukaryotes share one crucial feature. They depend on the unusual properties of a long twisted molecule called DNA, short for deoxyribonucleic acid. DNA is the molecule of life, for it possesses two properties that are literally vital. First, it carries the coded instructions needed to build and maintain the body it lives in. Secondly, and more important, it can copy itself. DNA can reproduce. That is the fundamental property of life, and DNA is the fundamental molecule of life.

The key to DNA's remarkable status is the structure of the molecule. The DNA story is by now very familiar, at least in outline, so much so that there is no need to retell it in detail here. (We do tell the more detailed story in our book *The Monkey Puzzle*.)[2] The essentials are that DNA is a double-stranded molecule, the two strands coiling about one another to form the renowned double helix, and each strand is a mirror image of the other. That is, each strand alone carries the information needed to build its partner. In the cell special enzymes, themselves coded by the DNA, unwind and separate the two strands, building a new complementary copy on each of the two old templates. Each strand of the old molecule gets a new partner and there are now two copies of the DNA where before there was only one. The DNA controls all the reactions that constitute the life of the cell. It is responsible for the manufacture of enzymes and other proteins, the compounds that maintain the processes of life. (The DNA has been called a blueprint, and we will sometimes refer to it as one, but this isn't strictly true. A blueprint looks something like the finished product, while DNA carries the information needed to build the product.) But as the cell grows that control becomes harder to achieve. Outlying posts become too far removed from the command. When that happens, the copying mechanism swings into action and duplicates one copy of the DNA, ready to begin again the cycle of growth and reproduction.

That, really, is all there is to prokaryote reproduction. The cell splits in two, generating two 'daughters' in place of the single 'parent'. As the old saw has it, bacteria multiply by dividing. We have made it all sound very simple, but of course it isn't. The dividing process, called cell fission, requires that the DNA be copied faithfully and that each daughter (sometimes there are more than two) gets a copy of the blueprints. There are the biomechanical problems of splitting the cell and rebuilding the walls, ensuring that the new walls do not trap bits of the DNA. And there is the whole question of timing and control, ensuring that the cell divides at a stage that will give the daughters adequate resources to get started on their own growth. But while there is much yet to be understood, there is also the fundamental fact that even today this is exactly how the majority of living things reproduce, by a single copying of the DNA and division of the cell. It is also the process by which all the body cells of a fully-developed human being are produced from a single fertilised egg. Certainly back in the Precambrian seas of 3.5 thousand million years ago it was the only method of reproduction that worked.

Even the simple business of cell fission, though, is a far cry from the very beginnings of life. The cell, all its enzymes and structures are coded for by the DNA, and all that coding serves but one ultimate function: to ensure that the DNA gets multiplied. Long before there were cells, when the pools of water that dotted the Earth's surface held rich stores of complex chemicals formed by the action of natural sources of energy on simpler compounds, there must have been a few molecules that were a mite more stable and could replicate themselves. Perhaps there was only one. These first primitive replicators used the chemicals in the primordial soup to construct new images of themselves.. Those that did so most efficiently, and most accurately, came to dominate the pool. Natural selection had begun in earnest.

Slowly the raw materials in the soup got used up, and the replicators had to turn elsewhere. Some perhaps cannibalised other replicators. Some became more active as enzymes, able to break down raw materials that other replicators could not use. Some, enclosed in a membrane, were protected from attack. Gradually the first functioning cells emerged from the replicator broth, and they did so, like the replicators before them, by virtue of superior reproduction. All the superstructure of life coded along the DNA—the cells, bodies, and even behaviour—exists for the benefit of that DNA. But the DNA exists only for itself. Molecular biologists can manufacture nonsense DNA by throwing code letters together at random, and cells will copy such DNA as readily as they copy meaningful messages. But nonsense DNA will never copy itself. The messages exist because they assist copying, and the manifestations of life are merely a reflection of that reproductive imperative.

Samuel Butler, the English author, was maliciously opposed to Darwin. He nevertheless hit the nail right on the head when he said 'a hen is only an egg's way of making another egg'.[3] The coding function of DNA is only the molecule's way of making another molecule of DNA.

The information that makes DNA the repository of its own future is carried in a four-letter code. The letters of the code are the so-called bases, different substances that are strung along the backbone of the DNA molecule. The sequence of letters along the DNA determines the structure of proteins, complex molecules made up of sub-units called amino acids which are strung together according to the DNA's instructions. The stretch of DNA that carries the coded instructions for the manufacture of a single protein is often called a gene, although there are other, sometimes confusing, definitions of 'gene'. The sequence of amino acids along a protein determines the protein's properties, and the properties of proteins enable the chemical reactions of life to take place. DNA is responsible for proteins, and proteins are responsible for biochemistry.

Four letters do not sound like much of an alphabet compared to the one we are using to communicate with you, but they are more than adequate to the task provided that there is room enough for the message. Indeed, computers use the simplest alphabet of all, the binary code with its two letters, on or off, yes or no, 1 or 0. Such a code is in one sense inefficient, because you need a set of five-letter strings of 1s and 0s ('words') to correspond to each of the twenty-six letters of the English alphabet, and even longer words if you want to include capitals, numbers, punctuation and so on. Our word-processing computers use eight-letter words; each one corresponds to a single character in English, and if we simply printed those out as a string of 1s and 0s this book would be eight times longer than it is. But what the binary code seems to lack in efficiency it makes up for in ease of processing, and our computers can find combinations of letters and shuffle them about very rapidly indeed.

The four-letter DNA code is effectively a compromise between the need for simplicity and the need for efficiency. A simple code is more likely to be copied accurately when DNA replicates, but it is more efficient to use short words in conveying instructions to the cell. The genetic code uses three-letter words to specify the twenty different amino acids that go to make up proteins, and there are other letter sequences which are like punctuation marks; these may be longer or shorter than three letters and are used to control the other messages. With the exception of a few minor aberrations in organelles such as mitochondria, the code itself is identical in all the living things that have been studied, and that suggests very strongly that all modern life has a single common ancestor. The code we see today is universal because it was the code that won the race way back in the Precambrian. There may well have been different replicator systems, perhaps even based on molecules other than DNA, but in the vigorous competition of early life one system, our system, came through, and it came through by virtue of its ability to reproduce itself faithfully, quickly, and efficiently.

There is a paradox here. Absolutely faithful copying, no matter how quickly or efficiently it is done, will not allow evolution. For evolutionary change to be possible there must be varieties to select among, and these varieties arise because replication is not always perfectly accurate. Sometimes the wrong base will accidentally be incorporated into the new strand, or a letter left out, or an extra one inserted. All these changes, called point mutations because they affect a single point on the DNA, can alter the structure of the proteins by encoding what is in effect a slightly different message. Mostly these changes will be harmful. The coded genetic messages have evolved to work and changes that scramble the code will usually make the mutated daughter cell less efficient than its parent.

Copying errors are not the only source of mutations; there are others that can happen at any time in the life of the DNA, not just at replication. Chemicals in the environment, cosmic rays, and especially ultraviolet light are all capable of disrupting the DNA. They may cause changes to the code, but they are even more likely physically to damage the DNA, so they are even more likely than point mutations to be harmful.

No matter what their cause, some—a very few—mutations are going to prove beneficial, making the mutant cell more efficient than its ancestor, and these are the ones that will be selected in evolution, but by far the majority are not, and the cell must somehow cope with the continual tendency of natural processes to corrupt its instructions. To do so, cells devised repair systems. They have proofreader enzymes, which scan along a newly synthesised double helix and check that the new strand matches (or rather mirrors) the old; if there is an error the proofreader enzyme chops out the offending base and replaces it with the correct one. (Of course even the best proofreaders are not perfect and some mistakes do get by.) Other enzymes repair the physical damage that is caused by ultraviolet light or other outside agencies, and even though ultraviolet light is no longer the threat to DNA that it once was, thanks to the protective atmospheric curtain of ozone in the stratosphere, almost all living organisms still have, to some degree, the enzymes needed to repair UV damage. This is yet another reminder of our Precambrian past. And in addition to proofreaders and repair enzymes, there is a whole suite of enzymes devoted to the process called recombination.

Recombination, at its most basic, is the welding of two different bits of DNA into a single entity. Specially constructed enzymes can cut a length of DNA from one place and stitch it in at another location entirely. So an early defence against damage could have been to scatter many copies of important messages along the DNA. Then, when one copy was damaged, it was no problem to find another copy and use it to repair the damaged stretch. These repair and recombination enzymes make possible a huge innovation—sex.

Bacterial sex, in outline, is almost as simple as cell fission. When two compatible bacteria find themselves next to one another they may form a thin living conduit between them. One of the bacteria, called the donor (or, by analogy, the male), then transfers some of its DNA through the conduit to the recipient (or female). The process is called conjugation, and afterwards the recipient can be thought of as the offspring of the union. The donor may give all its DNA to the recipient, or it may pass only a short stretch; there is no rule about the amount of DNA passed over, and unlike plants and animals the offspring rarely gets exactly half of its DNA from each parent. After conjugation the recipient may use its DNA repair and recombination enzymes to splice the received DNA and its own DNA into one long strand. The donor cell, if it gives away too much of its DNA, ceases to exist. Recombination, permitted by the existence of repair enzymes, thus allowed bacteria to create more variety, to bring together genes from different individuals into one body.

But why should this give the daughter an evolutionary advantage? As an example, think of some bacterium that causes disease in man, say a *Streptococcus*, which can give you a nasty sore throat. Doctors can treat the sore throat by prescribing an antibiotic like penicillin. This effectively changes the environment of the bacteria, making it lethal to most of the organisms. There is, however, a mutation that can save the *Streptococci* by making them resistant to penicillin. The problem, for them, is that the mutation is very rare, occurring on average just once every million times the DNA replicates. If the infection already includes a few specimens that harbour such a resistance gene, then those individuals will be selected and our throat will now be home for a resistant population. The sore throat may well clear up anyway, and it is not until the next infection, when the doctor tries penicillin again, that we realise that the original *Streptococci* have been replaced by the penicillin-resistant form.

Now the doctor uses another drug, say tetracycline, and again the bacteria succumb. As with penicillin, there are mutations that will confer resistance to tetracycline, and for the sake of argument we can assume that these too will crop up at a rate of one in a million. Obviously any *Streptococcus* that had both resistances would do very well indeed, but for that to happen the two mutations have to arise in the descendants of a single individual. The survivors of one mutation, who have no special advantage when there is no anti-biotic around, must mutate again for the other resistance, and the chances of that are two in a million million. (Two because either resistance mutation could happen first.) Two in a million million is a very slim chance.

Those are the odds for an asexual *Streptococcus*. For a sexual species the odds are very different. An individual resistant to penicillin could mate with one resistant to tetracycline and their offspring would be doubly resistant. The odds are not so easy to calculate, because they depend on more than simply the rate of mutation. Obviously the mutations need to crop up often enough to stand a good chance of being incorporated with one another. In practice this means either very frequent mutations or a very large popula-tion, conditions that may be true of bacteria in some cases. What-ever the exact odds, they are certainly less than 1,000,000,000,000 to 2, and probably quite close to 1,000,000 to 2. That difference, of making the doubly resistant bug almost a million times more easily with sex as without it, is a huge advantage indeed, and it is fortunate for us that bacterial recombination is not more frequent than it is. (It is interesting, though, that the genes for antibiotic resistance are often carried on small extra loops of DNA called plasmids, and these plasmids often also carry genes that promote their own spread by making the bacterium unusually likely to mate.) Resistant strains, given a competitive edge by unwise use of antibiotics, are already an enormous problem without the extra spectre of super-bugs that have, thanks to sex, accumulated resistance to many antibiotics.

The case of the resistant *Streptococci* dramatically illustrates the way that sex can bring sets of genes together, and this is what Fisher was getting at. A sexual species is more likely to survive a change in the environment because it can come up with new genetic combinations. This ability of sex to create new combinations of genes is often touted as the sole reason for its existence. That may be so in prokaryotes, but it is by no means the whole story.

We can imagine circumstances in which sex may be beneficial to prokaryotes, but in fact sex is very rare. To find it on anything like a regular basis we have to look among the eukaryotes.

The evolutionary origins of the eukaryotes are something of a mystery; most biologists agree that they evolved from prokaryotes, but they do not agree on the details. We could, for our purposes, simply assume the existence of eukaryotes, with sex, and continue from there. To look at the origin of eukaryotes is a slight digression, but one that we think illuminates the origin of sexual reproduction. So where did the eukaryotes come from? One hypothesis is that the nucleus, that most characteristic of eukaryote possessions, began as an internal membrane in a prokaryote, and that the other internal organelles arose by being pinched off from the nuclear membrane. But the favoured hypothesis, which is coming to be accepted by an increasing majority of people, is the symbiotic theory. This, which owes so much to the ground-breaking and proselytising efforts of Boston University's Professor Lynn Margulis, states that the various organelles that distinguish eukaryotes are the modified descendants of prokaryotes that were once, back in the dim reaches of the late Precambrian, free living.[4]

Mitochondria, for example, bear an uncanny similarity to bacteria, in particular to the aerobic bacteria that had evolved the ability to use the poisonous oxygen being put out by the blue-green algae. Some of those bacteria could well have taken up with other, anaerobic, bacteria. The host cell provided the aerobes with a ready source of food, in the form of the waste products of its own incomplete metabolism, and the aerobe returned the gift as energy-rich molecules made by burning those wastes in a fire of oxygen. The two came eventually to depend totally on one another in the relationship called symbiosis, a biological arrangement which benefits both partners. Chloroplasts, which house the photosynthetic apparatus, are likewise now believed to be the remnants of blue-green algae, prokaryotes with the ability to trap sunlight. Here the deal is energy in exchange for protection and raw materials.

The symbiotic theory has much evidence going for it, and is widely accepted, but surprisingly perhaps it does not offer a symbiotic origin for the nucleus. Such an origin has been proposed but it leaves too many questions unanswered. If the nucleus is the remnant of an invading prokaryote, where is the host cell's DNA? It is inconceivable that there should be no trace of it, for there are still traces of nucleic acids that can be found in the other organelles; those traces are part of the evidence for the symbiotic theory. Then again, the idea of the nucleus as a symbiont does not explain the very close co-ordination between the nucleus and the cytoplasm. Margulis offers two possible reasons for the evolution of the nucleus, both of which may be true and neither of which sees the nucleus as a symbiont.

It could be that the primary function of the nucleus was to keep the DNA from becoming too tangled. Some bacteria have a structure, the mesosome, which is a sort of infolding of the cell wall and to which the DNA attaches. When the cell divides the mesosome does so too, and each daughter strand of DNA attaches to one of the two mesosomes, so that each offspring gets one set of DNA. If the mesosome were to break away from the outer cell wall it could envelop the DNA completely and be very like a nucleus. The other idea for the origin of the nucleus is that it evolved because it protected the nucleic acids from the harmful effects of oxygen. Life evolved on an Earth where oxygen was very scarce, and this was probably a pre-requisite for life to emerge because oxygen is a very reactive element, able to break down complex molecules, including DNA. A membrane that kept oxygen away from the DNA would certainly be a great boon. The nuclear membrane does this. But regardless of the reasons why it evolved, the nucleus made it possible to package more DNA into the cell and still ensure that it got shared out equally at each division; to do that required a third kind of symbiont, one called the undulipodium.

Undulipodium means literally wavy foot, and it is the name Lynn Margulis gave to a whole class of seemingly very diverse organelles. (Each of them has a perfectly good name already, and the word undulipodium is useful only because it draws attention to their common features, rather than as a useful new word; we will not be using it much.) Perhaps the most obvious undulipodia are the cilia and flagellae, thread-like structures that stick out of cells and either move the cell through the liquid it lives in or, if the cell is fixed, move a surface layer of liquid past the cell. (Flagellae are really no more than long cilia; their detailed structure is identical, and you can just as happily think of cilia as short flagellae.) The cells in your nose and windpipe are covered with cilia, microscopic 'hairs' that waft the mucus, which traps dust and bacteria, in a never-ending stream towards the mouth. Many single-celled organisms are covered with row upon row of cilia that oar the organism through the water like a many-tiered Roman galley. Cilia and flagellae share a common internal structure. Sliced across, they generally have nine bundles of tubes arranged in a circle around a hub of two similar bundles, rather like a cartwheel. The bundles are fibres made of a protein called tubulin, and they can expand and contract. Wherever you find things moving inside a cell you find tubulin, and very often the circle of nine bundles too. All those structures, Margulis believes, are derived from free-living bacteria, the spirochaetes, that began by hitching a ride on an early eukaryote and became so thoroughly symbiotic that their free-living past is now hard to credit. Indeed, in fairness to critics we must admit that while most biologists are agreed that microtubules, as they are called, share a common origin, especially those that display the $9 + 2$ or $9 + 0$ arrangement (in some structures the two central bundles are missing), they do not agree that the common origin was anything like a free-living spirochaete.

Spirochaetes are long slender bacteria that corkscrew through their surroundings with great speed. The most familiar spirochaete bacterium, if not from experience then at least in theory, is *Treponema pallidum*, the organism that causes syphilis, but there are plenty of others. Some of those others are found in association with large single-celled creatures (protists), such as one called *Myxotricha paradoxa*, that live in the hind gut of various species of termite. This is a perfect place for such an organism, readily supplied with food by the termite and relatively safe, but there is one drawback. The organism must avoid being expelled when the termite defecates.[5] To do that it needs to stay near the top end of the hind gut, but its own powers of movement are fairly limited. Spirochaetes, however, come to the beast's rescue. They attach to the cell wall and, corkscrewing in unison, drive their host through the termite's gut. The organism stays inside its safe home, and the spirochaete takes the protist's leavings (which are in turn the termite's).

The existence of these symbionts is just one plank in Margulis' platform; there are many others and we believe that she will prove to be correct. But until we return to the sperm's propellor, also an undulipodium, we must now concentrate on another related structure that plays a central role in sexual reproduction.

When a prokaryote divides, its DNA most likely simply attaches to the inside of the cell wall and is carried passively into the daughter cells. The need to avoid entanglement is probably one factor that keeps the length of the DNA, and hence the complexity of the organism, low. Eukaryotes have an altogether different system for apportioning their genetic material, one that has been called the dance of the chromosomes. Chromosomes are yet another difference between prokaryotes and eukaryotes: in prokaryotes the DNA forms a single naked circle; in eukaryotes the DNA binds with special proteins to form a complex called chromatin and it is the DNA and its associated proteins that make up each chromosome. (People do refer to a bacterium's single strand of DNA as its chromosome, and although this is forgivable it is strictly incorrect.) The number of chromosomes varies from species to species, although all members of a species have the same number. A human being has 46 chromosomes, a fruitfly 8, and some ferns more than 600. You might think that copying 600 bits of DNA and ensuring that each daughter cell gets one copy of each would be even more of a headache than keeping a single long strand untangled, but it isn't, thanks to an organelle called the centriole.

The normal process of cell division in eukaryotes is called mitosis, and it really does resemble a dance. If you were to watch active growing cells under a suitable microscope, this is what you would see. For a long time, while the cell is growing, you would see nothing, just a constant streaming traffic in the cytoplasm. In particular the nucleus, with its cargo of chromosomes, would be a more or less featureless blob. Unseen, however, the DNA is being duplicated. When that is done the chromosomes begin to contract and thicken, and the nucleus comes to resemble a tangled ball of wool with a few distinct threads visible. The threads become thicker and shorter, and you may be able to pick out a slightly different looking region on each called the centromere. At the same time as the chromosomes are becoming more distinct, the centriole is beginning to divide. The single centriole of a resting or growing cell looks a little like a star, with short microtubule fibres radiating from a hub. Seen in detail, in an electron microscope, there is the telltale arrangement of nine bundles in a circle; the centriole, according to Lynn Margulis, is a descendant of the spirochaetes that became undulipodia. The centriole divides in two, and the two move around to opposite poles of the nucleus, stretching a so-called spindle of microtubules between them. The chromosomes are by now quite visible and you can see that each is composed of two threads, or chromatids, held together at the centromere. The nuclear membrane begins to dissolve, and this signals the end of the first part of mitosis, the prophase.

In the next stage, called metaphase, the centromeres seem to line up across the equator of the spindle. The chromatids themselves are still quite disorganised, but there seems to be a definite attachment between the centromere and the fibres of the spindle. So far, the dance has seemed chaotic, but now comes a stately progression. In each chromosome, the centromere holding the two chromatids together splits along its length, and each half starts moving back towards the centrioles at either end of the spindle. This is the start of the anaphase, and as the centromeres move to the poles each pulls its chromatid after it. The paired chromatids are separated, one member of each pair going to one centriole and the other to the other. The centriole has thus achieved a perfectly equitable distribution of genetic material. The rest of the cell begins to divide in half, during the telophase. A new membrane forms around the chromosomes in each daughter cell to reconstitute the nucleus, and the chromosomes once again become thin and indistinct. Ordinary cell division, mitosis, is complete, and thanks to the intercedence of the centriole and its spindle each daughter cell has a complete copy of the instruction manual.

At this point we need to think about chromosomes in a little more detail. They are called chromosomes because they take up coloured stains well, and if you look at the thickened chromosomes of a cell in prophase you will notice that they are banded across with light and dark stripes. You will notice that some chromosomes seem to have the same pattern as others. Indeed, it turns out that every chromosome has an identical partner, every one, that is, except the so-called sex chromosomes. But the others, the autosomes, definitely come in pairs. We cannot be sure how this came about, but one guess seems to be that it might have been a piece of cannibalism. When resources were low and times got hard, an early eukaryote might have swallowed up a member of its own species. Normally, such an event would be followed by the digestion of the food, breaking it down into its component chemicals. But suppose that the DNA was not digested, the cell would then have a double complement of DNA. This would give it two sets of instructions, and might provide copies of instructions that had been missing. These two factors would tend to make the doubly-endowed cell more efficient, but only as long as times are hard. When conditions improve there would be selective pressure on each set of genes to discard the other and get on with a new life of its own; if there are enough resources, each set of genes will do best without the other. This is exactly what happens today with some of the single-celled organisms, but the process is deliberate rather than cannibalistic.

One example is the protist called *Chlamydomonas*, one of those creatures that confused early biologists because it has two flagellae that move it around, like an animal, and chloroplasts that trap sunlight, like a plant. *Chlamydomonas* needs a supply of ammonia in its water, and as long as this is plentiful it reproduces by straight-forward fission. When the ammonia level drops, the organism turns to a different mechanism. Two individuals, passing one another in the water, will suddenly join their flagellae together and come to rest face to face, as it were. One, the male (or, more neutrally, +) strain, puts out a thin cytoplasmic tube that connects the two individuals. This gets wider and wider and pulls the two cells together, resulting in a single 'double' cell. The flagellae then come unstuck and the joined organisms swim off under the power of their four flagellae. They can stay like this for quite some time, continuing to make what use they can of the remaining nutrients, but after a time the double organism forms a tough coat around itself and waits for a favourable change in the environment. The organism is very resistant in this state, and some specimens have lasted four years or more. When conditions improve the two parental sets of DNA first duplicate and then separate, resulting in four offspring that swim out of the protective coat to start a new round of asexual reproduction.

Chlamydomonas typifies one feature of sexual reproduction. There is an alternation between cells that contain pairs of chromosomes and

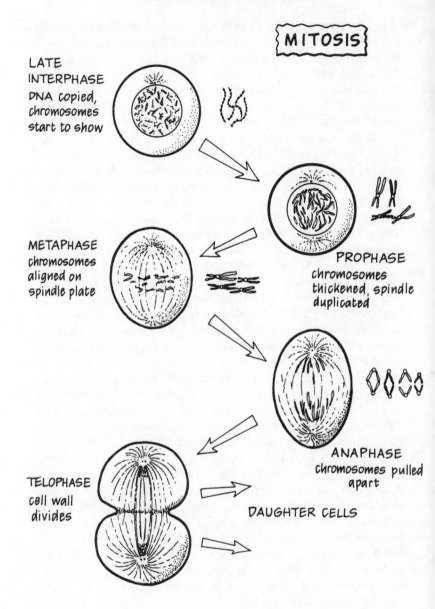

MITOSIS

LATE
INTERPHASE
DNA copied,
chromosomes
start to show

METAPHASE
chromosomes
aligned on
spindle plate

PROPHASE
chromosomes
thickened, spindle
duplicated

ANAPHASE
chromosomes pulled
apart

TELOPHASE
cell wall
divides

DAUGHTER CELLS

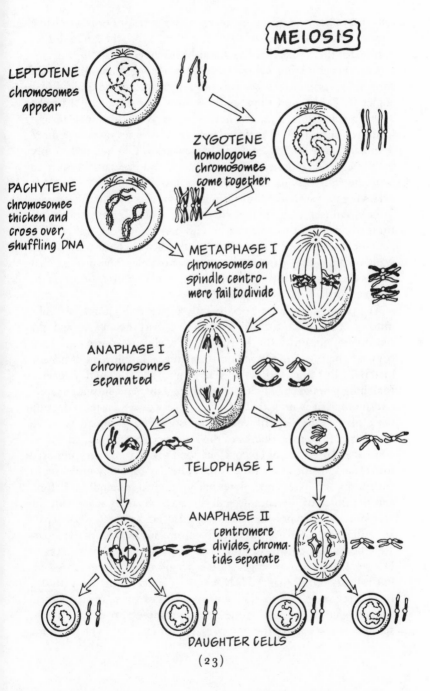

MEIOSIS

LEPTOTENE
chromosomes
appear

ZYGOTENE
homologous
chromosomes
come together

PACHYTENE
chromosomes
thicken and
cross over,
shuffling DNA

METAPHASE I
chromosomes on
spindle centro-
mere fail to divide

ANAPHASE I
chromosomes
separated

TELOPHASE I

ANAPHASE II
centromere
divides, chroma-
tids separate

DAUGHTER CELLS

(23)

cells that contain single chromosomes. In the case of organisms like *Chlamydomonas* it is the single chromosome type, the haploid, that dominates the life cycle. The fused haploid cells make up the so-called diploid resting spore, which has a double complement of chromosomes, but as soon as conditions improve the diploid first copies its DNA and then splits up into four new haploid cells. There seems to be a progression as we move from more ancient forms to more modern forms; the diploid becomes more and more dominant. Our bodies are composed entirely of diploid cells. Only the sex cells, egg and sperm, are haploid, and they quickly fuse to form the diploid zygote that will grow into a new person.

Having two sets of chromosomes is obviously a good thing under some circumstances, and we will explore some of the reasons later. But early organisms had evolved with just a single set, and while a back-up copy might be useful when times were hard they would want to ditch the spare set as soon as possible. The process that makes this possible is called meiosis, or reduction division. It is also the process that makes sex possible.

At first meiosis, which occurs only in sex cells, looks very like mitosis. The chromosomes thicken and become visible and the centriole divides to form the spindle. The chromosomes have been copied as before, and the cell now contains a double load of genetic material. But then something new and slightly odd happens. Matching pairs of chromosomes come together and entwine around one another. It is now that the key process of sexual reproduction takes place. Large chunks of chromosome are swapped between members of the pair, thanks to the activity of a group of enzymes. The enzymes are the old recombination tools that prokaryotes used for repair, but the effect now is to create a completely novel set of chromosomes. The centromeres line up across the spindle as before, and the fibres of the spindle pull the chromosomes apart. But the centromeres have not themselves divided, and so instead of separating the paired chromatids of each chromosome, the spindle separates the paired chromosomes. The result is two diploid sets of DNA. These then undergo another round of division that is very like mitosis except that the DNA is not duplicated before it begins. In this second division the centriole divides once again to form another spindle, and this time the centromere also divides so the spindle now separates the two paired chromosomes. The result is a set of four haploid cells, each containing one copy of each chromosome, and because of crossing over and recombination each chromosome in each of the cells is a unique amalgam of the equivalent parental pair.

If it weren't for meiosis, there could be no possibility of sex playing a continuing part in evolution. Sex is the fusion of genetic material from two different organisms. If it were to continue in each generation the amount of DNA would double up each time and the cell would quickly be completely overloaded with genetic instructions. Instead the amount of DNA is halved *before* the next sexual generation is produced. There is always an alternation between diploid cells and haploid cells; either type can form the main body of the organism, growing and reproducing asexually (mitotically), but if the body is diploid then meiosis will be used to produce special sex cells, and if the body is haploid then after the fusion of two bodies there will be meiosis to recreate new haploid bodies.

Merely doubling and halving the genetic material, however, is unlikely to be of much benefit. What really counts is the genetic shuffling that goes on in meiosis. That shuffling, presumably, is the reason why sex and meiosis are so widespread. But before we consider genetic mixing we should look briefly at the evolutionary origins of mitosis and meiosis.

Mitosis almost certainly came first; without a method of duplicating and sharing out the chromosomes there can be no need for a special type of division to halve the number of chromosomes in each cell. We have seen that the centriole, spindle and centromere play a central role in the process, and we have also seen that the centriole and spindle are probably the remnants of a free-living bacterium. If we imagine the early days of the partnership, we can see that it would be of mutual benefit to both the host and its spirochaetes if, when the host cell reproduced, the daughters received both a complete set of the DNA and their own spirochaetes. Indeed a spirochaete that could help its host achieve this distribution of DNA would do very well, because its success relies on its host's. So there is selective pressure on both partners in the symbiosis to ensure that reproduction is faultless.

The host is incapable of actively moving the chromosomes in the cell; it relies on the spirochaete for all powers of movement. Those spirochaetes that today live as symbionts, for example on the protist

Myxotricha paradoxica, are believed to have a special site on the protist's wall that they recognise and attach to. Those recognition sites are coded for by spirochaete genes, not genes in the protist. What if the centromere is not part of the original host's DNA at all, but a signal from the spirochaete to itself? We know that bits of DNA are forever being moved around from one site to another, and it is entirely reasonable that a bit of DNA specifying the attachment site could move from the spirochaete's DNA to the host's. The effect would be an enormous increase in the fidelity of reproduction, because the spindle fibres would recognise that site, the centromere, and attach to it. Provided the centromere divides when the chromosomes divide, the host is assured of a mechanism for partitioning its DNA, and the spirochaete is assured of a complete set of DNA to build a working host.

This story of the evolution of mitosis is naturally somewhat speculative, but it does make sense. It probably took a long time for the system to emerge, perhaps as much as a thousand million years, but that is a lot of generations for the cells in which mitosis evolved. Although the story is complicated there was enough time for natural selection to get it right. So important is mitosis to life that the pressure to get it right must be immense.

If mitosis is the spirochaete's way of ensuring that its own offspring end up with a perfectly equipped host offspring, what was meiosis for originally, and how did it evolve? We don't know, but we can hazard a guess. Fused cells, as we mentioned, are probably a good thing when times are hard because they offer more information to enable the organisms to cope with the hardship. But when the living is easy again they are more of a burden to move about. Besides, each was originally an individual and one can imagine that each would want to dissolve the partnership as soon as it was no longer absolutely necessary. So any mutations that would halve the amount of DNA would be selected for. We have seen that the only difference between mitosis and meiosis is that in the first division of meiosis the centromere does not divide. And we've seen that the centromere is probably part of the centriole and spindle, not the host's DNA. So a simple mutation, which has the effect of preventing one division of the centromere, achieves the goal of halving the DNA. And that simple mutation has taken place in DNA that doesn't really belong to the DNA being halved, it belongs to a creature that was once a free-living bacterium.

So much for the origins of mitosis and meiosis; their importance is that they allow an organism regularly to indulge in sexual reproduction by enabling it to shuffle its chromosomes. We now need to look at the chromosomes, and at what shuffling them means.

Each chromosome consists of a string of DNA bound up with proteins. Not all the DNA may be important; in fact it seems that less than ten per cent of the DNA carries genetic messages that are vital to the organism, but that ten per cent is divided up into discrete lumps called genes. Each gene codes for a specific protein, which may be a structural protein, or an enzyme, or a molecule that exerts some sort of control upon the cell machinery. So the organism is the final product of all its genes working together. Each gene has its particular place on a chromosome, called its locus, and geneticists have developed techniques to discover the whereabouts of many genes. But the genetic code at one locus on a chromosome may be slightly different from the sequence at the same locus on that chromosome in another member of the same species. The different versions of a gene that may be found at one locus are called the alleles of that gene. A gene may have just one allele, or two, or even more.

The two sequences may produce different proteins, and these may show up as some recognisable difference between the two organisms. For example, at the locus of the gene for making one part of haemoglobin, the red blood pigment that carries oxygen round the body, most adults have a particular sequence of about 500 bases. Some individuals, however, have a sequence in the same place that differs by just one letter. The result is that their haemoglobin differs by one amino acid and because this one interferes with the haemoglobin's job it is not nearly as efficient. Most individuals have the normal, or 'wild-type', allele at the globin gene locus, but a few have the different allele, called the 'sickle' globin allele because their red blood cells collapse into the shape of a sickle. Strictly speaking, one should always call the versions of a gene that occupy a particular locus the alleles of the gene at that locus. But this can be cumbersome and you will often come across the word gene being used to mean allele and (less frequently) locus.

The important thing about diploid organisms is that each cell has two copies of every gene, one on one chromosome and one on the other. The alleles at each locus may be the same, in which case the organism is said to be homozygous for that gene, or they may be different, in which case the organism is heterozygous. Sometimes one allele is 'dominant' over the other. Brown eyes, for example, are dominant over blue; this means that if a person has one brown-eye gene (now we are using the word to mean allele) and one blue-eye gene then that person's eyes will be brown. But the blue-eye gene is still there. In the next generation it may find itself sharing a cell with another blue-eye gene, in which case the eyes will be blue. This introduces another important distinction. The genotype of an organism is its complete genetic make-up, its full set of instructions. But because some of those instructions lie dormant, or recessive, like the blue-eye gene, the organism's outward appearance is not simply the sum of its parts. The outward appearance, the sum of those genes actually expressed, is called the phenotype. (The genotype and the phenotype are linked, of course, because one depends on the other, but there is a great deal more that goes to make up the phenotype than the genetic instructions alone.) It is because eukaryotes have diploid cells, with different alleles for many genes, that they can use sex and recombination to create new genetic packages.

When two gametes fuse, they bring together an equal genetic contribution—one chromosome of each pair—from the two parents. The new individual eventually breeds, and produces its own gametes by means of meiosis. In doing so it produces an absolutely new combination of genes along the chromosomes. This is because in the first phase of meiosis the process called crossing over occurs.

Crossing over is literally that. The pair of homologous chromosomes are drawn together until they lie side by side. Each chromosome has already been duplicated, so there are four chromatids, and the chromatids twine around each other. Enzymes come along and snip the chromatids where they cross, and other enzymes then repair the break, but in the repair the broken bits of one chromatid are rejoined to the chromatids of the other chromosome. In the simplest such recombination there is just a single break and the ends of the two chromatids are swapped, but there are often occasions on which there are two or more crossings over and a complicated exchange of DNA.

Crossing over is an almost universal feature of meiosis; there are some organisms, such as the male fruitfly, that do without it, but they are exceptional. Its effect is to mingle the parental genes into a new and unique combination. To see just how unique, consider the average human chromosome. This carries somewhere between 10,000 and 1,000,000 genes. (We would need 800,000 of our Apple computers to store the information carried on a single average chromosome. This entire book is less than about 50 computersfull.) Recombination can occur between any two genes (and within genes too, but we'll ignore that for now), so that two parental chromosomes can recombine into, say, 100,000 different offspring. There are 23 pairs of chromosomes, so that at this level one diploid cell could give rise to the truly staggering number of 10^{115} different gametes. (100,000 combinations of 23 chromosomes.) Astronomers estimate that in the entire visible Universe, all the stars of all the galaxies, there are altogether roughly 10^{80} fundamental particles—protons, neutrons and electrons.[6] So it would take 10^{35} *Universes* like our own to provide one such particle to represent every possible unique human being. That's an almost unimaginably large number in itself, and yet it is not the number of universes that we are concerned with, but the number of particles in all those universes put together. When the gametes from two individuals fuse we add yet another layer of individuality, with the result that we can safely say that no two people (apart from identical twins, who sprang from a single egg) share the same genotype.

So crossing over is a powerful source of variety, simply by recombining bits of the parental genome into a new genome to set before natural selection. It is for this reason, incidentally, that some biologists speak of the gene as the unit of selection. Genes come in packages called bodies, but every time those bodies reproduce their genes are shuffled into new combinations. The package that is one body's genotype is broken up, and the only level at which units of DNA survive is at the level of the gene. Even chromosomes last only as long as the body they inhabit. So while individuals, the phenotypes of specific genotypes, live and reproduce and die, recombination means that only genes survive from one generation to the next. Anything that keeps genes that work well together from splitting up may be favoured, but so long as recombination of any sort takes place the unit of selection will not be the entire genotype. Indeed, one of the definitions of a gene that Richard Dawkins, author of *The Selfish Gene*, has used is that it is the largest stretch of DNA that survives intact for several generations.[7]

Quite apart from its 'legitimate' role in producing variation in this way, crossing over and recombination add a further layer of variation by their occasional mistake. Sometimes the DNA gets looped during recombination, so that a length of code is inserted into its partner backwards. This is called an inversion, and it can affect the way the code is translated. Sometimes a chunk is lost, or inserted in the wrong place, again affecting the code. An entirely new chromosome may be formed when one is cut and not rejoined, or when crossing over unites two chromosomes from different pairs. All these events have happened in our own recent past. We share more than 99 per cent of our DNA with our nearest relatives, the chimpanzee and gorilla. But while we have twenty-three pairs of chromosomes they have twenty-four pairs each. Either two of theirs joined to form one of ours, or one of ours split to form two of theirs. Such is the accuracy of modern biochemical techniques that we know with certainty that our chromosome pair number 2 is equivalent to two pairs of the chimpanzee's chromosomes; most likely it broke during the split of chimp and gorilla from man. We also know that there are some parts of the chromosome that are inverted between man, chimpanzee and gorilla.

The predominant feature of sex, then, is a shuffling of the genetic hand. That shuffling can be achieved because the cells of eukaryotes have two separate ways of dividing. Mitosis always duplicates the cell and its contents exactly: if a cell with paired chromosomes divides by mitosis the result will be two cells with paired chromosomes; if a haploid cell divides by mitosis, the result will be two haploid cells. Meiosis is reduction division; it occurs only in diploid cells and gives rise only to haploid cells. Mitosis and meiosis both depend on the centriole and centromeres, which are probably remnants of free-living spirochaete bacteria. It is a sobering thought that the entire apparatus of sexual reproduction might be no more than a mistake, the result of one centromere, long ago, failing to divide when it should have. But the mistake was clearly a good one, for natural selection seized on the opportunity and now the vast majority of living things are capable of taking advantage of it. It enabled meiosis, and meiosis enabled genes to shuffle themselves into new combinations.

So prevalent is this genetic mixing, especially among the species we are easily aware of, that we tend to feel that it must be a good thing. If something has evolved, and been maintained, then we tend to assume that it carries some benefit. But think of our own appendix. This is a so-called vestigial organ, no longer of any use to us. A rabbit could not survive without its appendix, but in humans this little pocket off the gut frequently poses a threat to life. We can assume that, were we never to interfere, natural selection would eventually either eliminate the appendix totally or else weed out the genes that make individuals prone to appendicitis, but at the moment the human species is still stuck with an organ that is worse than useless. The same could be true of sex. Or it might be that sex, unlike the appendix, does confer some benefits. We know that sex, through crossing over, enables the genetic hand to be shuffled between each generation's game. But remember that the shuffle involves an enormous sacrifice on the part of the female; half her reproductive output is wasted. And remember too that, unless there is something funny about the rules, a hand that wins one game ought to win the next. So why throw away a winning hand?

WHAT IS SEX FOR?

Natural selection is like a meticulous accountant. If the benefits of doing things in a particular fashion outweigh the costs, no matter by how little, that way of doing things will be favoured. We know that sexual reproduction imposes an enormous cost on females, the cost of producing sons, which halves the return on a sexual female's investment. There are other costs too. So it is reasonable to ask what sorts of benefits there might be to offset those costs. If we can identify the benefits we will be well pleased at having solved this particular puzzle, but we may discover that in some cases there are no counterbalancing benefits; in those species sex is barely hanging on. A shift to asexual reproduction could easily vanquish it.

One of the commonest arguments is that sex exists because it enables evolution to go much faster. This it does by enabling favourable mutations to be combined together in a single body and spread through the population. In an asexual species favourable mutations can only accumulate in the descendants of one clone, while sex will bring them together from different individuals. This is an attractive argument, one that we have already dealt with by comparing a sexual and an asexual bacterium. There we showed that the sexual species would probably do better because it could become resistant to two antibiotics more quickly than an asexual species could. In fact, we were cheating with that example, because the bacteria have such vast populations that any mutation would be almost certain to arise relatively quickly. (If sex did make a difference to bacteria, they would use it far more often than they do.) That is the biggest problem with this particular argument; to get a difference between the sexual and asexual groups, the size of the sexual group needs to be large enough so that the mutations are indeed present in two different organisms. If the population is small, then the sexual population, like the asexual, will simply have to wait for the new mutation to arise, and by the time this has happened the first favourable mutation will have spread through the whole population anyway. As a rough rule of thumb, the population needs to be about ten times 'larger' than the chance of a mutation. In other words, if there is a one in a million chance of some mutation happening, the population would need to be about 10 million for sex to make any difference to the speed at which favourable mutations would accumulate. And that seems a little unlikely.

This is one problem with the 'go-faster' explanation of sex. There is another. As we have said, recombination is a double-edged sword. What sex brings together, it will also break apart. Recombination allows new sets of genes to be offered up to natural selection; it also ensures that those sets will be broken up the next time they are sexually shuffled. If you have a winning combination, how much better simply to copy it by cloning.

Another aspect to this kind of explanation of sex is one that considers the effects of sex on a whole lineage of related organisms. Because sex allows for variety, it enables species to respond to environmental change more readily than if they were asexual. That means that organisms with sex are more likely to evolve into different species than organisms without sex. Asexual species are likely to go extinct rather than branch. So the overwhelming preponderance of sex might be a reflection of the better survival and evolutionary branching of groups that can perform sex.

These two arguments, that sex enables faster evolution and that it promotes speciation, are the most common explanations. We have hinted at some of the difficulties, and will return to them, but first we should note that they both take a very long-term view. Sex is seen as advantageous in evolutionary time, even though it loses out in the short term. That may be so, but can we not find advantages in the here and now?

George Williams, at Stony Brook, has adopted a straightforward approach to the problem of sex.[8] He takes as his starting point the observation that many life forms alternate between sexual and asexual reproduction. They may reproduce by cloning for many 'generations' but they then indulge in a bout of sex. The aphids that infest rose bushes are like this. The females who arrive on the bush grow genetically identical clones within themselves, and those daughters may already be growing granddaughters before they are even born, three generations supported by one efficient set of mouth parts and the rose's supply of food. But then, come the winter, a change in the environment, the female aphids produce winged males and females, which mate sexually and lay eggs. Or think of strawberry plants, which cover the ground by spreading asexually produced plantlets on the ends of runners, but also produce flowers that set sexually produced seeds. Williams argues that there must be some mutation that would be capable of suppressing the sexual stage completely, and that if this were to save the organism the costs of sex then it would spread very quickly.

The common dandelion is a simple example. Dandelions do not reproduce sexually, but produce seeds which carry the same genetic message as the parent, and, indeed, as each other. Dandelions come in a few varieties, descended from sexual ancestors, but today the members of most of those varieties are no more than clones. Out of more than 2000 species of dandelion only 50 reproduce sexually and they are restricted to small regions of West and Central Asia and the Mediterranean.[9] The dandelion can hardly be regarded as an unsuccessful plant, as any gardener struggling to keep a patch of lawn free of them will testify. Nor is it restricted in where it will grow; members of one clone are found as far afield as Greenland and Florida. But the dandelion's success does not, today, depend on sexual reproduction. If conditions changed—if a new Ice Age rolled across the Northern Hemisphere, perhaps—then dandelions might feel the pinch, losing the habitats in which they thrive and being unable to adapt to the changing conditions. Then, sex could be advantageous; but today, as far as the vast majority of dandelions are concerned, it is not worth it.

This example also throws another sidelight on evolution, worth a slight detour from our main argument. If dandelions do not reproduce sexually, they have no need for pollination and no need to attract insects to carry their pollen from flower to flower. Yet one of the most distinctive things about the dandelion is its bright yellow-orange flower. What can it be for? Quite simply, it serves no purpose, but is a reminder that the dandelion is descended from sexual ancestors. Many generations ago bright flowers to attract insect pollinators and ensure reproduction were essential to those ancestors. But once a genetic pattern becomes fixed in a line that reproduces without sex, evolution goes so slowly that, for all practical purposes, it ceases in that line. Mutations are so rare that there is no realistic prospect of eliminating the waste of resources involved in the production of those attractive, but useless, flowers.

The first mutant dandelion to reproduce asexually (which probably arose quite recently) had insect-attracting flowers, and so all dandelions today have coloured flowers, whether they need them or not. In this case, the advantages of asexual reproduction, even with the useless appendage of a bright yellow flower, obviously outweigh the disadvantages of sex. But the very fact that so many organisms continue to use sex points to a powerful short-term advantage, one that at least matches, and perhaps exceeds, the twofold advantage of cloning.

The aphid's life gives an insight into what the advantage of sex might be. A rose bush is a hugely abundant source of food. Any aphids that happen to land on it will be up to their ears in food. They will reproduce, each as fast as it can, and slowly the fastest growing clone will edge the others out by sheer force of numbers. That clone will be the winner of the race to exploit that rose bush, and it is the winner because it is more perfectly adapted to the exact conditions on that rose bush than any of the other aphids who happened to land there. But when the resources represented by that particular rose bush have been exhausted, it will be time to send out pioneers to seek new sites. The successful clone has two options. She can send out lots of identical clones, in the hope that one of them will land on a rose bush exactly like the exhausted one, where its genetic endowment will ensure a measure of success. Or she can send her investment out in the form of several slightly different variants, the products of sexual reproduction, in the hope that one of them will land on a rose bush to which it is perfectly suited. The strategy that will pay best will be dictated by the likelihood of finding an identical rose bush. If the chances are good, send out the clones. (Which, of course, is what she does while filling a particular rose bush with her offspring.) But if the pioneers are likely to find themselves in a different environment, then it is probably better to make each slightly different and hope that, in the race to exhaust a fresh source of supply, your offspring, despite being only half yours, is the one that is ideally suited to that supply.

It is in this context that Williams developed his oft-quoted analogy of the lottery. Asexual reproduction is like buying a whole stack of identical lottery tickets; if that number is a winner, you will be a winner. Sexual reproduction is buying half as many tickets, but each with a different number; if the winning number is uncertain this gives you a better chance than a stack of Xerox copies. Williams went on to apply this type of thinking to a diversity of different lifestyles, not simply the aphid.

The strawberry, for example, cannot move freely about within the resource, as the aphid can, but it can spread and hope to colonise new lands. The strawberry plant spreads by making clonal copies of itself, and these will continue to spread as long as they are better adapted than neighbouring clones, which are probably different. In this way the strawberry clone will come to cover that part of the habitat that it is best adapted to. Rather than the discrete spatial boundaries that limit the aphid's spread, it is shifts in environmental conditions that limit the strawberry's growth. When it comes to long-distance spread, however, the strawberry is in exactly the same position as the aphid. The environment that a seed finds itself in is most unlikely to be identical to the environment it came from, so variation among offspring gives the strawberry the best chance of establishing further successful clones elsewhere.

Another case that Williams examines is the one he calls the elm-oyster model. Here, the problem is that hundreds or even thousands of juveniles can occupy the space that will eventually be taken up by just one adult. Oyster larvae are minute compared to the full-grown adult, and the carpet of seedlings below an elm gives just a hint of the competition between them to become established. An elm seedling may find itself with no competition for a while, but as it grows it will come under the influence of neighbouring seedlings that are also growing. The more successful will crowd out the less, eventually killing them, and will continue to grow. As they do so they come into contact with yet more seedlings, and the competition now is tougher because those seedlings too have won small local competitions. The cost of meiosis is just one small factor buried beneath all that extra selection. The eventual winner has had to conquer thousands of rivals in order to grow to maturity, and a variety of different competitors is the best way to ensure that one of them might win. Because the prize is finite—only one elm can occupy the space—there is nothing to be gained from having multiple copies of the winning genotype. Neither elm nor oyster ever reproduces asexually. They are exclusively sexual, and it is the fierce competition between juveniles that makes them so.

It is not simply the unpredictability of the environment that makes the new combinations afforded by sex successful. Nor is it the competition between different species. If that were so, we should expect to find a preponderance of sexual reproduction among species that are good at colonising new areas, whereas in fact many weeds are asexual. Rather, it is the competition *between siblings*. If each offspring went to a different new patch, sex and cloning would be equivalent, but because several offspring usually end up in the same patch, the parents are far better off with variety between their pioneers, so that in each patch there is a better chance that some new combination of their genes with another individual's will be the winner.

Williams considers three different types of reproduction system that involve sex: the aphid alternates a bout of asexual multiplications with a sexual generation; the strawberry spreads across short distances with clones, but uses sex to go further afield; and the elm does not use clonal reproduction at all, but produces millions of seeds. These models can each be seen as extensions of an idea Williams called the sisyphean genotype. Sisyphus is the character in Greek mythology who laboriously pushes a boulder to the top of a hill. Just as he reaches the summit, the boulder crashes down the hill and he has to begin his labour again. Williams' point is that the fittest individuals, those best able to reproduce under the prevailing circumstances, would owe their success to a rather fortuitous combination of genes, and that combination would probably not be among the elite in the next generation. Hence, the sisyphean genotype has to be recombined anew in every generation, just as Sisyphus had to keep rolling his stone up the hill.

Each of his examples is a Sisyphus of a sort, trying to make at least a contribution to the most successful individuals of the next generation. The common factor in all is what Williams calls a very high level of zygote-to-zygote increase, or ZZI. (The ZZI is the number of offspring that a single organism is capable of producing; in species that alternate sexual and asexual reproduction it is the number of offspring produced sexually by all the clonal descendants of the original individual.) To give you an idea of what 'very high' means, consider not the aphid but the water flea, or *Daphnia*, which has a very similar life cycle. The growing season, during which the animals reproduce asexually, lasts about six months, and during its six-week lifespan an average female will produce about 40 young.

At the end of the growing season *Daphnia* lays eggs that will survive the winter and will be capable of sexual reproduction. If all the asexual offspring were to survive and reproduce, by the end of the season a single zygote could produce more than 10 million offspring. A female oyster over her lifetime may produce at least 100 million young. In every case where there seems to be an advantage to sex, it is because of the intense competition for resources between the offspring of a single individual. Indeed, most of Williams' mathematical models simply will not work if there are not enough offspring to compete, and that brings us to a major problem; many living things, perhaps all the ones that interest us, and certainly our own species, do not have nearly enough offspring. Competition between siblings is not strong enough to take evolutionary advantage of the variety that sex affords. They would be far better off, according to the mathematical model, putting the same effort into twice as many asexual offspring.

The world's most fertile woman, according to the *Guinness Book of Records*, had 69 children, at least 67 of which survived infancy.[10] Even so, that is so far below the numbers needed by Williams' model as to be absurd. If competition for resources were the only factor, very few animals, and especially not the exceedingly slow-breeding human animal, would be sexual. Williams' conclusion is that 'sex must be disadvantageous' in 'mammals, birds and many insects'.[11] The clear implication is that these species must have evolved from an ancestor that enjoyed very high fecundity and in whom sexual reproduction completely ousted asexual. For birds and mammals (and reptiles and amphibians too) that ancestor might have been a fish, or it might have been even older, a protochordate. As we shall see, where the ability to reproduce asexually has arisen in one of these low-fecundity species, it is generally exclusive; the clonal form is very successful and leaves no room for a sexual phase. One can conclude that human sex today is very definitely maladaptive, but then why has natural selection not been able to eliminate it?

The answer is that, as a result of many millions of years of evolution when sex was advantageous, there are now formidable obstacles that prevent its loss. One is that most organisms have completely lost the ability to bud off whole new versions of themselves. This is not quite so true of plants, which retain unspecialised

cells that can form the basis of a new, physically separate but genetically identical, individual, and is probably one reason why a return
to asexual reproduction is quite common among low-fecundity
plants. But animals, by and large, are not able to bud off clones,
because as the zygote develops into the adult the cells become
specialised and differentiated into the various tissues of the adult.
Even those cells that continue to proliferate madly, like the cells that
completely renew the lining of your gut every forty-eight hours, are
trapped by their fate, able to produce endless quantities of new gut
cells but not cells that will in turn develop into new individuals.

The exception, of course, is the embryo itself. Before development has proceeded too far it is quite capable of dividing into two or
more parts that will grow into wholes. This is cloning, pure and
simple, and it is very good for the embryo. A genome that finds itself
in an egg that forms twins has effectively doubled its chances. But it
does the mother no good at all. She has already paid the price of
meiosis, and genetically identical offspring incur the costs of asexual
reproduction without the benefits. The extra nutritional burden of
twins may be one factor that discourages twinning, but especially in
animals with large litters the added cost of a doubled embryo is not
large. The benefit, to the embryo, is considerable. But despite the
obvious imbalance in benefits between mother and embryo, the
mother seems to win this struggle, and twinning is comparatively
rare among mammals. Only armadillos go in for it on a regular basis.
(Zygotes that find themselves in an egg provisioned with yolk presumably can seldom afford to build two offspring from a single
supply of nourishment.)

Another obstacle to asexual reproduction is created by the very
diploidy that sex requires. Having two sets of genetic instructions
means that a duff copy on one chromosome can be compensated for
by a good copy on the other. The harmful recessive mutation will not
be expressed, but nor will it be eliminated, so all diploid organisms
carry an invisible genetic load of mutated stretches of code. If an
animal chooses to become a haploid asexual, the harmful mutations
will not be covered by a working copy of the gene, and so the
offspring are liable to suffer very high mortality. Any opportunity to
reconstitute the protective diploid state would be seized, and the
organism would very quickly revert to being a normal sexual
diploid.

The answer to this problem might be to stay diploid but reproduce asexually. The trouble with this option is that it seems to
need a whole series of mutations to happen at the same time.
Meiosis must be suppressed or cancelled in some way. The egg
must resist fertilisation by sperm, which if it took place would
almost certainly lead to an unworkable number of chromosomes.
And the egg must be able to start and maintain its own development without either the signal provided by the sperm's entry or
the mitotic spindle that the sperm usually provides. And yet
despite the need for a seemingly impossible series of co-ordinated
mutations, eggs do arise that are capable of parthenogenetic
development, and one can artificially select for individuals in
which parthenogenetic eggs have become quite common.

In fruitflies perhaps one in a thousand eggs will develop without being fertilised. Astute selection can increase this figure to
more than one in 17, but only if the females are kept apart from
males.[12] Were the female flies allowed to mate, the six per cent
of eggs that are capable of unaided development would probably
be killed by the addition of the male's chromosomes. Turkeys
too can be selected for parthenogenesis.[13] A strain was
developed in which many unfertilised eggs showed some
development, and one in several hundred reached maturity. Curi-
ously, all the birds produced were male; that parthenogenetic
females should give rise to males means that the offspring cannot
be identical copies of their mother, though the exact details are
not known.

Turkeys and fruitflies can be turned into asexual species, or at
least made more asexual than they were before, but there are also,
despite all the obstacles, quite a few vertebrate species that are
predominantly asexual. (There are also many invertebrates without sex, but they will not concern us much here.) There are fish
that have abandoned sex, though some of them retain a curious
vestige of their sexual past, and amphibians too that multiply
asexually. And in the southwest of northern America there is a
flourishing group of lizards that reproduces entirely asexually.
In none of these animals, however, is sexual reproduction an
option; that is, these species are exclusively asexual and do not,
like the aphid, have the option of using sex when they need to.
Williams sees this fact as 'decisive evidence'[14] that sex is a bad

idea and would be selected against in practically all vertebrates. If it were not, sexual and asexual would be able to co-exist side by side.

Biologists recognise two main types of asexual reproduction in diploid organisms. One is called arrhenotoky, and involves producing males from unfertilised eggs and females in the usual way. It is common among social insects, where the special arrangement (males are haploid and females diploid) leads to odd kinship relations and a predisposition to become highly social. The other is called thelytoky, and is the production of females from unfertilised eggs. An egg can be made to develop into an adult female in two ways; either meiosis is entirely suppressed and the offspring is an identical copy of the parent, or else meiosis takes place but the reduction in chromosomes is made good by some special process. The first method, when there is no change in the genome, is called apomixis. The second is called automixis.

Apomixis is a fine method for producing identical offspring. If meiosis doesn't occur, the egg is effectively just a bit of the parent and will develop into an exact clone. Automixis, however, is more of a problem. The trouble is that no matter what steps are taken to overcome the halving of chromosomes during meiosis, the offspring will not be identical to the parent, and nor will they enjoy the protection of diploidy to the same extent. This is because crossing over and recombination after the duplication of the chromosome shuffle the mother's genes; if she now puts two sets of recombined chromosomes together in an egg, the chances are that some of the genes will have come originally from the same chromosome. The offspring will thus be homozygous for genes that the mother may have been heterozygous for. In the extreme case, when the mother simply duplicates one haploid set of chromosomes after meiosis, the offspring will immediately be homozygous at every locus. Whether it is all or just a few genes that are made homozygous, the result is that the offspring is exposed to all the dangers of the lethal recessive genes accumulated as part of the normal genetic load, and so it is most unlikely that an organism that has been reproducing sexually for some time will be able to give rise to viable offspring by automictic thelytoky. It can happen, but it is very rare indeed. Thelytoky with apomixis, by contrast, is relatively common.

Arrhenotoky will not lead to long-term asexual reproduction because the males are not themselves capable of laying eggs; but because it exposes the genes to selection in haploid bodies, it can pave the way for automictic thelytokous asexual reproduction by ensuring that the genome does not contain too many lethal recessive mutations. The few rare cases in which females produce daughters from unfertilised eggs that have none the less been through meiosis are each thought to be evolved from an arrhenotokous ancestor.

Theory, then, says that while asexual reproduction may be a highly desirable state of affairs for many animals, and probably all vertebrates, it is by no means easy to achieve. A look at some of the species that have, as it were, gone back to their reproductive roots is very enlightening.[15] One of the most interesting is a little fish called the Amazon molly (*Poecilia formosa*) which has almost, but not quite, done away with males. The Amazon molly is thought to have arisen from a hybrid of two closely related sexual species. It reproduces asexually sure enough, laying unfertilised eggs that grow into exact genetic replicas of the mother. Indeed, no male Amazon mollys have ever been found. But the females retain a curious reminder that their species was once sexual. In order to trigger the growth of the egg into a new clone, the egg must be penetrated by a sperm. And to get the necessary sperm the emancipated Amazon molly has to dupe a male of one of the closely related 'parental' species into mating with her. He gets absolutely nothing out of the deal; the genetic material in his sperm is totally ignored by the egg's genes. The molly has almost all the benefits of asexual reproduction, but still she has to find a male and get him to mate with her. Doubtless a female who could abandon even this last trace of erstwhile sexuality would do even better than her sisters. She would be able to explore territories where there were no males, for example, but there is scant chance of this happening, for the molly is now set in a rigid mould; having abandoned sexual reproduction she has also abandoned the chance of combining a new, 'sperm-free' mutation with the one that gave rise to her line, and will have to wait for such a rearrangement to happen to one of her descendants. Even so, and even bearing in mind that by human standards fish produce vast numbers of offspring, the Amazon molly has found it cost effective to abandon sexual reproduction.

The same need to find a male afflicts another of the asexual vertebrates, the salamander *Amblystoma*. Here again, there are two ordinary diploid sexual species, but two asexual types, probably the results of misguided mating. The parthenogenetic forms are triploid females, having a diploid set from one of the sexual species and a haploid set from the other, and like the Amazon molly they need to find a male and mate with him, for the eggs must be penetrated by a sperm before they will start to develop. It seems that the asexual salamander is slightly further down the road to complete female emancipation than the Amazon molly, because one does occasionally find all-female populations away from any males, and these are capable of parthenogenesis without even the minor mechanical stimulation provided by a sperm.

(There is an even more bizzare form of asexual reproduction in another fish, *Poecoliopsis*. As in *Amblystoma*, there are two completely normal diploid sexual species and a couple of parthenogenetic types that are triploid. But there are also diploid all-female types. These females mate with males, and the male genes are expressed in the offspring, but when the time comes for meiosis, only the female's genes go forward into the eggs.)

Parthenogenesis in vertebrates is paradoxical. If Williams' arguments about the benefits of sex are correct, asexual reproduction should be very common. But it is not. And yet, when it does occur, it seems to wipe sexual reproduction out completely. So the benefits of parthenogenesis are clear, and when it happens mere sex doesn't stand a chance. But the obstacles put up by eons of sexual evolution are formidable. Are those obstacles the only reason why asexual reproduction is rare? Perhaps not, for it is as well to remember that almost all our knowledge of evolution comes from fossils, and it is very difficult to tell how a fossil reproduced when it was alive. Williams was looking for a short-term advantage to sex. He found it, in the need to avoid competition between offspring. But if there is a long-term advantage to sex, one that, for example, helps a lineage to survive by making it more likely to give rise to new species, then we have another explanation for the rarity of asexual vertebrates. They are committing what Williams calls 'phylogenetic suicide'.[16] Asexual reproduction may be a very good thing in the here and now, avoiding the two-fold cost of making males, but it may doom the species to an early extinction.

At any moment there may be literally hundreds of species that are on the verge of breaking through from sexual to asexual. For all we know human beings may be one such, and there may already have

been true virgin births. When the breakthrough to asexual reproduction does occur, it spreads rapidly and wipes out the sexual
ancestor. But without the long-term benefits of sex, the asexual
species is prey to any sudden change in its circumstances. It is very
vulnerable to extinction. Sexual species, by contrast, perhaps find it
easier to adapt and so are more likely to survive, and more likely to
branch. Thus the prevalance of sexual reproduction among the
snapshot of species that grabs our attention now is not a reflection of
the quick benefits of sex; those benefits accrue only to much more
prolific multipliers. It is, rather, a reflection of the sad fact that
asexual reproduction *is* better in the short-term, but doesn't last
long. Hence, it doesn't often appear in a single frame from the
movie of life. The prevalence of sex must therefore be either a
hangover from earlier days or have something to do with long-term
benefits (or both).

So far, we have mentioned two possible long-term benefits to
sex. One is that it enables species to evolve more quickly, thus
keeping up with changes in the environment. The other takes an
even longer perspective and says that species with sex, because they
can avoid extinction, give rise to new species more readily, and so
groups that have sex will persist and proliferate. They may both be
false. It is quite clear that sexual reproduction does indeed make it
possible for a species to show almost limitless variability without
any input either in the form of mutations or the arrival of related
individuals adapted to slightly different conditions. Evolution is
indeed faster with sex than without. George Williams, however,
turns this observation on its head and asks why, then, evolution is
so slow.

Bring an animal or plant into the laboratory and select for some
character, and the species will respond very quickly. You can increase the number of bristles on a fruitfly, or the scent of a rose, in a
very few generations. But look at the fossil record and it seems that
species change only very slowly, certainly under natural selection
they evolve at a rate much slower than they are capable of when man
makes artificial selections. This could be because the environment
simply does not require them to change more quickly, but if that
were so they would abandon the evolutionary speed of sex for the
increased returns of cloning. Or it could be because in the laboratory the scientist selects just one characteristic, and quickly uses up

any genetic variability in that character, whereas in the wild natural selection acts on many things at once and has to balance the sifting out of variants against the creation of new ones by mutation. But either way the problem remains; if sex is good for fast evolution, why is evolution among sexual species so slow?

According to Williams, we are looking at the problem from the wrong end. Most biologists tend to think that extinction takes place when an animal cannot keep up with changes in the environment. Williams says that 'extinction occurs not because an organism loses its adaptation to an ecological niche, but because its niche becomes untenable'.[17] The animal may be perfectly adapted to its niche, but the niche may vanish for other reasons. One example Williams mentions is the green turtle that nests on Ascension island in the middle of the South Atlantic. The adults feed on turtle grass off the coast of South and Central America, but every two years or so they make the monumental journey across the Atlantic to nest on Ascension. They are probably perfectly adapted to this life, and would continue to weather changes in, say, salinity, or currents, or nutrition. But if Ascension were to be eroded away that population of turtles, despite having the advantages of sex and recombination, would in all likelihood go extinct. 'If . . . the island disappears,' Williams says, 'the last turtle to lay her eggs there may still be extremely well adapted to her niche, but it is a niche that in the next generation will permit a total of zero occupants.'[18]

In Williams' view, sex *retards* adaptation. The force of recombination that breaks up existing favourable hands is, he thinks, more important than that which brings new hands together. And this, so far from preventing evolution, enhances the survival of groups with sex. There are always a few oddballs out on the fringes who play the game slightly differently—the turtle who lays her eggs somewhere else, for example. When times change, the oddballs may survive while the main line goes extinct. Because sexual species do not go extinct as readily, they are more likely to speciate and give rise to further sexual species. If organisms really did track the environment as quickly and as closely as they can in the laboratory, they could find themselves exquisitely well adapted to a way of life that is itself about to end, with no prospect of escape from the trap of overspecialisation.

It is very difficult to judge the merits of Williams' arguments as compared to the more orthodox view. It is appealling, true, but that is not enough. John Maynard Smith, of the University of Sussex, has developed mathematical models which show that under the right conditions sexual species certainly will change faster on the basis of existing variability, spread new mutations through the population more quickly, and follow changes in the environment more closely. But is that what keeps sex going in the long-term? We don't know.

There are just two more arguments about the long-term value of sex that we must deal with. They go by the name of Muller's ratchet and the Red Queen hypothesis.

Muller's ratchet comes from the geneticist H. J. Muller, who was one of the first to suggest, in the 1930s, that sex owes its existence to its ability to speed up evolution.[19] Muller's ratchet is a more recent invention, dating to 1964. What he notes is that an asexual species can never get rid of harmful mutations. In that sense, mutations are like a ratchet; they can increase, but never decrease (except in the unlikely event of the mutation exactly reversing itself). A sexual species, however, because it can recombine genomes, has the opportunity to rid itself of bad genes. Occasionally offspring will contain as their new genetic hand a preponderance of harmful genes. They will die, but the species as a whole will do better because it will have filtered some of the harmful copies from the gene pool. Such a mechanism probably does work in the real world, especially where each genome is likely to experience less than one mutation during its lifetime, and where that mutation is not going to be very harmful. What Muller's ratchet really means is that any population will be able to replicate more DNA without accumulating errors if it uses sex and recombination than if it merely copies the DNA as faithfully as possible. More DNA, of course, means a potential for greater complexity. And the especially nice thing about this conclusion is that it brings us full circle. As John Maynard Smith explains, 'it is now widely accepted that the genes responsible for recombination evolved in the first place because of their role in DNA repair. What follows from Muller's argument is that recombination itself functions as a form of repair.'[20]

So much for Muller's ratchet; it enables species to use sex to lift the pawl and rewind the ratchet. What of the Red Queen? It was the Red Queen who explained to Alice, in her adventures through the looking glass, that 'it takes all the running you can do, to keep in the same place'.[21] To Leigh Van Valen, an evolutionist at the University of Chicago, this is a perfect analogy of evolution.[22] Van Valen perceived a law in the fossil record, which was that any genus in a group, say any bony fish, seemed to have a constant probability of dying, going extinct, at any time. Van Valen explained that it was not the inanimate environment that was important but the living environment, the other species that share an area. Any change for the better in one of these species would automatically be a change for the worse for all the other species. If one species becomes a better competitor, the others are bound to suffer as a result. Hence, all species must evolve as fast as they can, just to stay on an even footing with all the others. Sex enables faster evolution, and so sex, like the Red Queen's frantic bursts of speed, is needed just to stay in the same place.

Between them, Muller's ratchet and Van Valen's Red Queen add yet further refinements to our knowledge of the costs and benefits of sex. Whether they are general phenomena, or apply only under certain stringent conditions, we cannot say. In common with most of the other models of sex we have looked at, they rely on changes in the environment to make sex worthwhile. But in mathematical models with realistic assumptions it is very hard to get these ideas to work, either because the population is too small or because the environment changes too slowly. Unsatisfactory though this is, in the short-term, it seems that sex can be a direct benefit to very prolific organisms whose offspring will compete among themselves for resources. In the longer term, sex may speed evolution and may also retard adaptation, both of which could promote the spread of sexual species at the expense of asexual species. But in the short-term asexual species, despite being doomed to an early evolutionary end, seem to win out in the battle with their sexual ancestors. All in all it seems that the business of creating a new individual from a mixture of two old individuals—for that is what sex is—is a remnant from earlier times.

Some species, like the Amazon molly, have managed to get rid of it. Human beings too might do better, in the sense of reproducing more effectively, if they could abandon sex (which means abandoning males), but that doesn't make it likely that we will undo all the biological inheritance and evolve away from sex. Martin Daly and Margo Wilson, two biologists at McMaster University in Ontario, have this to say about the matter: 'Asexual reproduction might indeed be a more selectively advantageous trait in people, could we but begin. Wings might come in handy too, but it is equally improbable that we will soon sprout them. Characteristics cannot evolve simply because they would be useful . . . We seem to be stuck with sex, and only a disenchanted few regret it.'[23]

Sex, as a method of reproduction, is of no clear advantage to us here and now. But what of gender? We are stuck with sex; are we also stuck with two different sexes?

WHY TWO SEXES?

In Fred Hoyle's novel *The Black Cloud* scientists establish radio communication with an intelligent being that takes the form of a huge cloud that travels between the stars. The cloud, which is essentially immortal, is greatly puzzled by the mechanics of human reproduction, and the human obsession with 'love'. Having been sent a representative sample of human literature to study, it points out that 'nearly forty per cent of literature is concerned with this subject'. The scientist speaking for the contact team tries to explain:

'Viewed from a wholly logical point of view the bearing and rearing of children is a thoroughly unattractive proposition. To a woman it means pain and endless worry. To a man it means extra work extending over many years to support his family. So, if we were wholly logical about sex, we should probably not bother to reproduce at all. Nature takes care of this by making us utterly and wholly irrational . . . it's probably the same with all the other animals too.'[24]

Hoyle talks of 'nature' arranging things, but we can understand better in terms of genes. The genes that inhabit our bodies don't 'care' about the pain, suffering and hard work those bodies have to go through, as long as copies of those genes are made and passed on to new bodies. Imagine a gene for logical behaviour arising. We all know people who do behave rationally, by Hoyle's yardstick, and avoid the pain and trouble of children. (Of course we do not mean to suggest that they have a gene for logical behaviour; this is by way of an example.) Fine for them, but what happens to the logical gene? Nothing. It quickly vanishes from the evolutionary stage. A gene for 'love', in Hoyle's use of the word, is, however, a big success. It ensures the strong pair bonding which is such an asset in a species where the offspring are weak and helpless for years, and need a lot of parental care. So the children of a loving couple have more chance of survival, more chance to reproduce in their turn and spread their genes still further. It is, in fact, quite straightforward to explain the phenomenon of love to the alien cloud.

But suppose it had asked a further question. It's easy to see the advantages of two parents being bonded by love to make the best possible home for their offspring. But why should those two parents be of different genders? Why, indeed, are there two sexes?

The scientist in the story would have had a lot more trouble answering that question, for it is very difficult to see much point to the two-sex system, especially where human beings are concerned today. The problem is that, like sex itself, the system of gender evolved a very long time ago, when it was distinctly advantageous, and we are stuck with it. Nature cannot backtrack on evolution and start afresh; new variations on the evolutionary theme are overwritten on top of existing blueprints. This has two effects. First, it means that natural selection is forever having to make do, turning old ideas to new purposes. François Jacob, a French Nobel Prize winner, describes nature as a tinker, making do and mending, finding new uses for old pots and pans.[25] A bird's wing is built of the same parts as a human arm, but the two constructions are used very differently. Unless some feature is actually detrimental to the survival of an individual it will still be passed from generation to generation even though it may have outlived its usefulness.

But before we can tackle the question 'why gender?', we need to know what gender is, even though the details of how gender is determined have no bearing on why it evolved. In the most fundamental terms, at the genetic level, the differences between male and female are easily distinguished. Every cell in the body of every normal human being contains a complement of forty-six chromosomes, twenty-three from each parent, arranged in pairs. As we saw in Chapter One, twenty-two of those pairs are closely matched and are concerned with the development and functioning of the body in which they reside; the two chromosomes that form the remaining, twenty-third 'pair' are not so closely matched to one another in appearance, but together determine the gender of their body. The sex chromosomes come in two varieties, called X and Y. The X chromosome is quite large, ranking seventh in order of size of the twenty-three, but the Y chromosome, which looks like an incomplete X, is the smallest of the set, one-fifth the size of the X.

When the twenty-third pair of chromosomes is XX, the body they inhabit is woman; an XY pair defines a man. Because of this arrangement, it is the father's contribution to a newly fertilised egg that defines its sex. The mother can contribute only an X chromosome to each of her eggs, but sperm from the father may carry either an X or a Y.

As long as there is a Y chromosome, the egg will develop as a male, and most fertilised eggs contain one of the two combinations XX or XY. Aberrant individuals have been born with 'extra' chromosomes in combinations such as XXY, XXX, even XXXXY. But no matter how many X chromosomes may be present, the individual develops as a male provided one Y is there. (There is no evidence for the widespread modern myth that individuals with two Y chromosomes, so-called XYY males, are more aggressive and especially prone to violent and criminal behaviour.) An egg without an X chromosome, by contrast, cannot develop at all, suggesting that in some sense the basic form is female, and that maleness is a modification of it.

Studies of the development of the fetus confirm this idea. Like all genetic material, the sex chromosomes send out their instructions as chemical messages; they control the production of enzymes, which in turn affect either local biochemical activity in the cell or produce biochemical changes throughout the body. But for the first six weeks after conception there is no sign of any development of the human fetus towards one sex or the other. Then, if the fetus is to become a baby boy, it begins to move along those lines. On the other hand, if the cells of the fetus carry the XX pair, development towards the mature female state begins only after several more weeks have passed. If the fetus shows no signs of maleness by six weeks, then it is definitely female. At every step down the line, the move towards maleness occurs before the corresponding move towards femaleness.

Studies carried out on other species elaborate on this picture. In cattle, farmers had been puzzled for centuries by the occurrence of 'freemartins', calves born with a mixture of male and female characteristics. In every case, such a calf is the twin of a normal male, and the explanation is that hormones produced by the developing male twin have travelled through the placenta to hijack the body of the female developing alongside. Because the female doesn't receive a full dose of male hormones from her twin, however, she turns into a semi-male. When male hormone is injected into a developing female fetus during the critical period within which sex is being determined, it develops as a male; but if gonads (testes or ovaries) are removed from either a male or a female fetus at the same stage of development, it develops as a female. The male hormones seem to suppress the female development as well as encouraging the development of male characteristics, which is why they have to get in first during development, to ensure that the fetus is not already too far down the road to becoming a female. But an embryo will develop as a female without either sex hormone being produced in its body.

(This account is true for mammals, but it isn't the whole story—see Chapter Five. Briefly, in birds it is males who are ZZ while females are ZW. And in reptiles like turtles and crocodiles (but not snakes) it seems that the temperature during incubation determines the sex of the infant that emerges from the nest. In the Mississippi alligator a hot egg becomes a female and a cool one a male. In some turtles the reverse is true. Many species of fish can change sex during their lives, usually switching from female to male as conditions dictate.[26] The XY system in mammals is probably the best understood, but it is as well to be aware that life can be very variable. In any case, how gender is determined is of no importance to why gender is determined or what its consequences are.)

The role of the Y chromosome is decisive in determining sex in mammals, but that is almost all it does. The X, unlike the Y, also carries other genetic information. Many studies have shown that several structural genes are carried on the X chromosome, but the only one definitely linked to the Y chromosome is a gene for hairy ears. And, of course, the so-called H-Y antigen, which is almost certainly the primary chemical switch that directs development onto the male path. The female has more genetic material than the male, but because one of the X chromosomes (chosen at random) is switched off in every cell this may not all be fully expressed.

This extra genetic material might help to explain why females are more rugged than males, and less prone to ailments of one kind or another. Although some 120 males are conceived for every 100 human females, just before birth the ratio has been reduced to 110:100 by the male's extra vulnerability to miscarriages, many caused by chromosomal abnormalities. In terms of live births males outnumber females by only 106 to 100, and the extra vulnerability of males continues throughout life so that by age 70 the ratio at conception is reversed and there are 120 women for every 100 men.[27]

Male babies are more prone to suffer complications, such as lack of oxygen supply to the brain, and men are more prone than women to many physical and mental ills. Women, in spite of the rigours of childbearing, have a greater life expectancy than men, and it has been suggested that this could be due to their extra genetic material.[28] This is unlikely, however, because male birds are the ones with the extra genes, and yet they suffer all the consequences of being male that beset humans.

Looked at another way, the vulnerability of males is the result of their being male. Interestingly, bodies that contain an XY pair, genetic males, don't differ from females if they don't have male hormones. The pashas of the Ottoman Empire helped us to understand this point. They used eunuchs to guard their harems, and the eunuchs enjoyed a longer lifespan than comparable servants who had not been castrated. More evidence on this point comes from the lunatic asylums of America. Until recently, it was accepted practice in some parts of the US to castrate certain inmates. These unfortunate individuals lived on average fourteen years longer than their intact fellows. And neutered cats live longer than intact toms.[29]

Something about testosterone, the male hormone, shortens the male's life. And testosterone is also responsible for the competitive, 'masculine' aspects of being male, as well as being associated with the presence of a Y chromosome.

There is a complicated web here that we must try to untangle. All the differences between male and female can be seen as the results of their different hormones, which in turn stem from their different chromosomes. If we pursue the chain of cause and effect resolutely we come to the ultimate evolutionary question. What is it that enables organisms with gender to succeed better than organisms without gender? The answer may be 'nothing'. Male and female may be inevitable consequences of sex, but before we get to this we want to repeat that, in some fundamental sense, women, like all female mammals, came first; the old Adam and Eve story is precisely wrong, even as an allegory. In allegorical terms, the story would make more sense if Eve came first, and Adam was an afterthought created out of a modified portion of her body. Males are simply modified females tailored to a particular role in the reproductive process. We have already hinted that the male's role has something to do with competition. But how did the distinction between the sexes arise in the first place?

We have to go back a long way into the history of life on Earth to tackle those questions. To recapitulate: somehow, back in the primordial soup of the Earth's oceans, or in some warm little pond, at least one—but perhaps only one—molecule acquired the trick of replication, making copies of itself by arranging chemical constituents from the soup in the correct order. Natural selection operated on the descendants of that molecule, conferring an evolutionary advantage on those that stored the chemical building blocks they required around themselves, in the first cells. These were much simpler structures than the cells in our bodies, just bags of DNA with little internal structure, and crucially lacking the central nucleus that is the heart of a more advanced cell. For this reason, they are known as prokaryotes, meaning 'pre-nuclear', while the kind of cell that makes up the bodies of all higher organisms is called a eukaryote.

The step from prokaryote to eukaryote is widely regarded as the most significant evolutionary development in the history of life on Earth. Eukaryotes contain many semi-autonomous parts within themselves, units specialised for the jobs of absorbing energy, for locomotion, and so on. All this flexibility enables cells to act together in multi-celled bodies, specialised for different jobs but all carrying the same genetic message. And just as large organisms are built up of many cells working together, so it seems that eukaryote cells are, in fact, assemblages of different kinds of prokaryote whose ancestors once led independent lives. As we have mentioned, this idea is associated with Lynn Margulis, of Boston University. To cut a long story short, she argues that as the 'free lunch' provided by the original chemical soup was very quickly used up and turned into living material by the many different forms of prokaryote that evolved long ago, these bacteria-like organisms turned their attention to one another.[30] The larger organisms could engulf smaller ones wholesale, and take over their chemical storehouses. 'Eating' had been invented, and natural selection would give an edge to the larger cells. At the same time, however, cells that could swim would experience a selection pressure to swim faster and avoid being eaten, while small cells that depended on capturing solar energy and turning it into chemicals would become more efficient at their own trade. Suppose, now, that in one encounter between a large browser and a small photosynthesiser the small cell, although engulfed, turns out to be indigestible. It stays inside the body of the large cell, but continues its old job of converting solar energy into chemical food. This could be a big plus for both cells—the large one gets energy, the small one avoids getting eaten by anything else. If the smaller cell could reproduce, by fission, inside its host, so that when the host itself divided there would be some smaller symbionts in each daughter cell, then a step down the road to eukaryotes would have been taken.

In fact, this particular step was probably one of the last to be taken down that road, although it makes too good an example to let that worry us. So symbiosis gives us multicellular eukaryotic organisms, and eukaryotic organisms enjoy the benefits of sex. But where did sex begin?

All the living things that you can see—trees, birds, flowers and people—are collections of eukaryotic cells. The prokaryotes survive today, indeed they are highly successful life forms, but as single-celled organisms they are invisible to the naked eye. They are the bacteria and their relations, the almost unchanged descendants of the oldest forms of life on Earth. We are descended from the same ancestors but in highly modified form.

Sexual reproduction is almost exclusively a preserve of eukaryotic organisms. Most prokaryotes reproduce asexually, by cell division or by budding off a smaller daughter cell from a larger parent. Some do engage in a form of sexual reproduction, with one cell passing on a portion of its DNA to another, but this does not involve passing on the full genetic code, just a portion of the available DNA. Even so, the importance of this development should not be ignored. After all, where did the variety of prokaryotic forms, the building blocks of eukaryotic cells, themselves come from? Partly from new mutations, to be sure, but also from mixing genes together. Sharing genetic material is, primarily, a way of producing a variety of genetic combinations, and therefore a variety of offspring. 'Sex among the bacteria may', as one writer has put it, 'have led to a rapid proliferation of different kinds of unicellular organisms.'[31] But in prokaryotic sex, there is never an equal contribution from both parents; in eukaryotic sex, there always is (apart from the differences between X and Y chromosomes already mentioned). Sex as we know it is eukaryotic sex, and it seems logical to see the development of sexual reproduction as part of the same process of symbiosis that, as Margulis describes, led to the development of eukaryotes themselves.

Nobody knows exactly how sex as we know it got started, but clearly it involved the coming together of two cells and the sharing of their DNA. One possibility is that this was the result of an attack on a fat browser by a small, speedy swimmer, in much the same way the viruses operate today. A virus is entirely parasitic on cellular life, unable to reproduce on its own, simply a DNA (or RNA) message wrapped in a protein coat. The virus penetrates a living cell and hijacks the machinery of the cell so that it turns out many copies of the virus before the cell itself dies. Could our speedy swimmer have done something similar in the Precambrian, invading a fat cell replete with the chemicals of life, and combining its own DNA with the fat cell's genetic material? Even if, virus-like, such a relationship originally turned out copies of the invader at the expense of the host, mutation might eventually have produced a mixing of DNA and thus offspring that had a mixture of parental properties. It's possible, but unlikely. Without sexual reproduction to provide variety, where did the sneaky swimmers come from? Who were the ancestors of the fat cells? And mutation on its own, as we have seen, is painfully slow, probably too slow for this version of events to be true. Doesn't it make more sense to see sex appearing first, and only then the amount of variety between cells that this scenario requires?

As soon as you start asking those questions, the pieces of the puzzle fall into place, and it becomes clear that, in all probability, the first sexual reproduction involved cells of more or less the same size that came together, perhaps as a result of trying to eat one another and finding, in each case, that it had bitten off more than it could chew. The first eukaryotic organisms to reproduce sexually, alternating fusion with the formation of gametes by meiosis, probably inherited this technique and reproduced without any distinction of gender. There was just one gender, and one type of gamete, although there may have been different mating types. Nevertheless, any gametes produced by one individual could fuse with one of those produced by any other individual (of the right type) to make a viable new individual. This is called isogamy, and the process is still used today by organisms such as some algae and fungi, which are regarded as primitive forms of multi-celled life.

Only some, perhaps very few, of the gametes produced in this way will meet a partner and become part of a new individual. The competition between gametes to find the partner without which their genetic message will not be reproduced applies intense selection pressure; anything that enhances the chances of a successful union will be seized upon, and the isogamous organisms would quickly change. As we explained briefly in our introduction, Geoffrey Parker, of Liverpool University, and his colleagues have developed a plausible scenario of the way in which natural selection will lead almost inevitably to the evolution of two, and only two, sexes from the initially isogamous ancestral form.[32]

We start with a primitive state in which there is only one sex, and each individual produces gametes that can each fuse with a gamete from any other individual to make a new individual. Success is when a gamete finds a partner; failure—absolute and irretrievable—is when a gamete fails to find a partner and its genetic material is lost. Taking this a little further, it's no good two gametes meeting and fusing if the resulting new individual doesn't survive to maturity and produce gametes of its own. But these are the only basic requirements for a gamete to be successful. It must meet another gamete, and the resulting fusion—a zygote—must survive to maturity.

One way to increase the chances of finding another gamete is to have a long life. Gametes that are well supplied with food will, therefore, have a better chance of achieving success. This attribute is doubly beneficial, for a good supply of food is also an essential requirement for development once two gametes have fused and begun to develop towards the mature adult form. In any natural process, there is variation, and we might imagine that initially our isogamous species would produce a range of gamete sizes, some bigger than average, some smaller, a distribution clustered about some mean value. As long as increased gamete size is an advantage, organisms that make slightly larger than average gametes will do best in the survival stakes, and will pass on their genes, including genes for gamete size, to their offspring. As the generations go by, there could be an upward drift in the mean size of gametes as a result.

But this is not the only factor at work in our original isogamous population. There is another way to ensure that a gamete meets a partner and fuses with it successfully. By sacrificing everything else for speed and mobility, a gamete could get ahead in the race to find a partner. As long as they can get about, smaller than average gametes will, therefore, also be at an advantage in the initial population. Of course, two smaller than average gametes that fuse to form a zygote will not be very well off. The zygote will be small, and may lack sufficient supplies for its full development. So there is a very strong selection pressure in favour of small gametes that can preferentially seek out large partners. As small gametes get smaller, and large ones get larger, the pressure becomes more intense; small gametes become completely useless to each other, and large ones a more and more valuable prize. A small gamete must fuse with a large one to be successful. A large gamete might, at this stage, still fuse success-fully with another large partner if it could find one. But large gametes cannot move easily, so the chance of two large, relatively immobile gametes finding one another before a small gamete latches on to each of them becomes increasingly remote as the two types become more distinct. The initial population, which pro-duced a range of gamete sizes centred on a mean, splits into two new populations, one of individuals that produce large gametes and one that produces small ones.

Two distinct strategies have emerged from the isogamous popu-lation. (Three simply would not work—selection would pull those in the middle to one end or the other.) One is to invest the available reproductive resources in a few large gametes, which we might as well now call eggs, for that is what they are. The other strategy is to invest the same resources in huge numbers of very mobile gametes—sperm. Neither strategy can be successful on its own, and once the process is in train selection acts to make sperm smaller and more mobile, eggs larger and better storehouses, until the limits of each strategy are reached. The two sexes have arisen in-evitably from an isogamous population, and the distinction between them is fundamental, remaining in their descendants today. Regardless of body size and outward characteristics, or genes and chromosomes, the fundamental distinction between male and female in all species that reproduce sexually is that males produce small gametes and females large ones.

From that inequity, everything else flows. The female, right from the word go, invests more in her offspring. Her reproductive potential is limited by her own efforts, by how much in the way of resources she can gather and channel into eggs. The male's direct investment, though, is cheap. He can manufacture millions of gametes at very little cost, and his reproductive potential is limited far more by what other males are doing, by the number of opportunities he has to impregnate a female and take advantage of her investment. That is fundamental to gender, and therefore of the evolution of sexual species. Martin Daly and Margo Wilson, looking at the evolution, long ago in the Precambrian seas, of anisogamy (sex involving different gametes) write that 'the quick little sperm can be said to parasitise the parental resources that [the female] provides'.[33] Putting it more bluntly, men are parasites on women.

Though striking, this quip is not quite accurate. As long as sexual reproduction is an advantage, as long as it helps to ensure the survival of genes, females still need the opportunities to recombine their genetic material in new arrangements, opportunities that can only be provided by mating with a male partner. And parental care by males decreases the females' costs. In any case, the simple mechanics of the process, thanks to millions of years of evolution, make men indispensable, and the male gamete still has a role to play. Where the human species is concerned, though, the quip may be more apt. If we are not sure that sexual reproduction is actually any advantage for us, we are saying that we are not sure that men are necessary at all. And at the same time technology is bringing us dramatically close to the day when it may be possible to use gametes—egg cells—from two distinct female individuals and persuade them to fuse into a viable, sexually produced zygote, thus getting the benefits of sex without the hassles of gender.

Already more than a hundred test tube babies have been produced by fertilising human eggs with human sperm in the laboratory (not actually in a test tube, but no matter; 'petri dish baby' doesn't have quite the same ring to it), then implanting the fertilised egg back in the mother's body. In other species, such as frogs, the nucleus has been removed from an egg cell, and the egg injected with the nucleus from an ordinary body cell of another frog. This produces a 'fertilised egg' that carries the same genetic code as the donor and develops into an identical replica of that frog. Implant many nuclei from one donor into many eggs in this way, and you have a horde of genetically identical frogs—clones. Indeed, simple mechanical stimulation, a prod with a sharp probe, will often start an unfertilised frog egg dividing, with no male contribution. Indeed, research on eggs removed from women for in-vitro fertilisation has revealed that some human eggs begin to divide spontaneously with no help from a sperm. It is by no means impossible that a combination of these techniques, plus some new ones, could either stimulate a human egg to divide without fertilisation or take two human egg cells from different women and persuade them to fuse into a viable zygote, ready for implantation back into the womb. Technology, as well as evolution, emphasises the redundancy of the male to the female members of our own species.

It all looks very different, of course, through male eyes and foreseeable technology doesn't look like being able to change things for men. Without the aid of a female, no male can reproduce, and without reproduction his genes die with him. Just as in the earliest evolution of gender, therefore, females remain a resource for which males compete. We shall see in the next chapter how this fundamental fact has moulded animal behaviour, but before going on to look at sex in the wild, we want to develop our theme that, although it is straightforward to understand how gender arose naturally, and why sex has proved an evolutionary advantage for countless species, including our own, it may well be that both have outlived their usefulness for the human species.

Sex can indeed be a benefit to the individual—when the individual is sending out offspring to seek and exploit new territory. As with other aspects of biological behaviour, this can be modelled mathematically, and on the basis of such models George Williams concludes that it works best when there are millions of pioneers and only a handful of survivors. If more than a very small proportion of the pioneers survive to breed in their new surroundings, then asexual reproduction remains the best method of passing on genetic information. These conclusions are borne out by studies of species (some of which we met in Chapter Two) that are capable of reproducing either sexually or asexually, depending on circumstances, and of those that have, partially or totally, abandoned sex today.

Some species get the best of both worlds. The greenfly that infests your roses and inspired one of Williams' models is a perfect example. When a female greenfly finds a juicy plant on which to feed, she does nothing but feed and reproduce, growing unfertilised eggs into clones inside her body. If the food suits the mother, it is bound to suit her offspring, who are simply copies of herself, and the greenfly population explodes. But it is a different story when the food supply begins to run out. Now, with insufficient food available, changes are triggered in the greenfly's reproduction process. Males as well as females are born, and they mate to produce a variety of sexually reproduced individuals. This variety of greenfly then sets off for pastures new. Many fall by the wayside, but each one that survives to find another juicy rose bush has a chance to start the cycle again.

This is a very efficient adaptation indeed. But where does it leave the rest of us—not just we humans, but all animals that reproduce sexually even though a high proportion of our offspring survive to breed and the pioneer effect is modest? Are we, and most of the animal kingdom, ill-adapted, breeding sexually when we would do better instead to grow copies of ourselves, by asexual reproduction?

In our view, and as explained in the previous chapter, that is indeed the case. Women would do better without sexual reproduction. Mankind has conquered the environment to an enormous degree, making the variety possible through sexual reproduction largely redundant. When a new Ice Age comes along, the successful members of our species won't be the ones with more hair, or more fat, but the ones with the most efficient technology to keep them warm. The most successful members of our species today—and by this we mean biological, not social, success, although often the two go together (see Chapter Six)—are almost certainly not those best suited to the old natural environment that shaped us, and culture counts for far more. Perhaps this is why books such as David Rorvik's fictional *In His Image* strike such a chord with us. Rorvik claims that the book tells the true story of a millionaire who arranged for the creation of a clone of himself; the book, despite scientific denials, was a great success. Do we know, without thinking about it, that asexual reproduction is a better bet today? Leaving aside the pleasure of sex for the sake of sex, we seem to be left with a clear deficit in our budget that no conscientious accountant would permit. Sex no longer pays. As Groucho Marx is supposed to have remarked when asked why he no longer fooled around with young girls (actually the quote is from a letter *to* Groucho), 'The screwing you get ain't worth the screwing you get.'[34]

If a woman appeared who could reproduce parthenogenetically, a theme taken up by several science fiction stories over the years, or if the technology of cloning became a reality, asexual reproduction could easily become the norm, although, again as spelled out in many of these stories, it might be best to keep a group of sexual breeders in reserve, a living gene bank available in case conditions change and pioneers are needed.[35] The benefits of sex may no longer be present, but the biology is. Man—more accurately, woman—has reached the point where, like the Amazon molly, she could go her own way. But we are stuck with sex, an attribute which is so bound up with the structure and development of our living bodies that it is very difficult for nature to 'un-evolve' it.

Stuck with sex as we are, we will spend the rest of this book examining the ways in which our method of reproduction has shaped our way of life. We have evolved through a succession of sexual ancestors for a thousand million years or more, and it would be foolish to deny the effect this has had on our present behaviour. And these effects can best be seen by looking first at the way sex affects the animal world in general.

SEX IN THE WILD

For some species, reproduction consists almost entirely of making gametes. True, there is the additional effort that may be needed to find a partner to fertilise your gametes, but with that done the young can be abandoned. Any effort beyond that needed to ensure fertilisation is extra. That extra is called parental behaviour, and it comes in many guises. Nest building and incubating are obviously parental, but so too is defending a territory, which then provides food and shelter for the young.

Because of the variety in parental behaviour, there is also a bewildering array of mating systems. Where two parents are needed to raise the young we are likely to find stable lasting bonds between a single pair—monogamy. But where a single parent (or none) can do the job the way is open for animals to have more than one mate—polygamy. And between those two extremes lies a spectrum of possibilities.

If nature really were the cosy confederacy people often imagine it to be, sex and reproduction would be a matter for mutual co-operation. Male and female would get together to ensure the survival of the species. That simply is not the case, for if it were the mating beaches of elephant seals would not run red with blood spilt in fights between males, and no male spider would ever be eaten by his mate. Each individual seeks to maximise the number of descendants it leaves, and that may mean competing directly with members of the same species and the same sex. The pacifist elephant seal, or the spider who passes up the chance of an extra meal, will not do as well as those who seize the opportunity. By virtue of the initial asymmetry between their gametes, the ways for males and females to achieve more offspring differ from the outset, and it is the resolution of that primal conflict in different ways that provides the variety we see around us.

The archetypal female is a careful nurturant mother. She gathers resources and channels them into her offspring, protecting her investment to ensure that it matures. The harder she works, the better she will do. The archetypal male, by contrast, is a profligate inseminator, competing with others of similar ilk for the opportunity to take advantage of as many mothers as possible. He does better by winning more mates. In some species the typical pattern does exist, and the male contributes only a package of genes to the next generation, but variants on that pattern are also common. Most of the studies of the biology of breeding have been carried out on birds. This is partly because they are easier to study, partly because their habits, being close to our own in many respects, made them attractive to early naturalists. Whatever the reasons for this bias, it means that most of our examples will be drawn from the world of birds.[36] We will, of course, refer to other types of animal where appropriate, with one notable exception; in this chapter, we are not interested in *Homo sapiens*. But much of the rest of the book will be taken up with an investigation of how the principles derived from other animals apply, as indeed they must, to our own species.

Typically, the male deserts the female, who raises their offspring on her own. Typically, that is, in mammals; in birds 95 to 97 per cent are monogamous, though a few do show the mammalian pattern. This is true, for example, of birds like the ruff, a member of the sandpiper family. Males congregate to form a group called a lek, and their curious booming calls ring out over the river marshes on which they breed. They compete with one another for tiny mating territories on the display ground, and females attracted to the lekking males prefer certain positions, often those near the centre of the crowd. A male will try avidly to court any female who wanders through his territory, but he will not pursue her into another male's area. If he is successful, he transfers his sperm to her egg; that is the end of his contribution.

All the alternatives to the typical pattern also occur. The opposite case, where the female deserts the male, who then performs all the parental duties, is much rarer. One reason that is often given for why it is rarer is that the female makes the bigger investment to start with and so is unlikely to abandon her investment. This explanation is wrong, because what matters is not the effort already put into raising young but the benefits to be had by redirecting future effort to, say, another brood. Richard Dawkins has called this mistaken type of reasoning the Concorde fallacy, after the expensive Anglo-French supersonic aircraft that proved to be something of a white elephant.[37] It is throwing good money after bad or, more brutally, sending in another platoon of soldiers so that our boys shall not have died in vain. What matters is not how much you have already spent, or lost, but how much you can expect to gain by starting a new enterprise as opposed to continuing the present one. Where parental behaviour is concerned, each partner can put the other into a cruel bind. If some parental care is needed, the first to desert forces the other to decide whether it should stay and look after the young. One parent may be able to manage, none would be a disaster, and usually it is the female who ends up being the caretaker.

The archetypal male can always gain more by inseminating a female, abandoning her, and then putting his effort into finding another female rather than looking after the offspring he has just created. This is not such an easy option for the female, not because she has already invested heavily in her eggs but because she is trapped by her own body. The fact of the matter is that in many animals fertilisation takes place within the female's body. This probably arose to protect the gametes and ensure that they did meet, but it means that the male gets first crack at abandoning his partner. (It also raises the spectre of being cuckolded, which we will return to later in this chapter.)

But there may be other good reasons for the male to stay with the female and protect the young, even if he doesn't participate in the work of actually rearing them. The African lion's way of life highlights just one aspect of the complex interplay of sexual roles in the matter of parental behaviour. Lions do not take direct care of the cubs; indeed many cubs die as a result of infanticidal males. But this, and other aspects of their life, makes sense.

Lions live in prides, which consist of males, females and young. Lions are often said to own the females, but this is misleading; the pride's core is a group of related females and their young, and it is the continuing line of females that survives through time. The females have with them at any one time a group of two or three adult males. Young males are thrown out of the pride before they can mate with their sisters or pose a threat to the adult males, but occasionally the males who dominate the pride will be challenged by outsiders, males ejected from other prides. If the newcomers succeed, one of the first things that happens is that cubs vanish. The reason is probably always infanticide, confirmed in a few cases when researchers saw a male with a dead and bloody cub in his mouth.

The immediate advantage of this to the lions is that it stimulates the females to become sexually receptive. Losing their cubs triggers the oestrus cycle and ensures that cubs will be born to the new pride males as soon as possible. Given their limited tenure of the pride this is obviously a good thing for them. But why do the lionesses permit infanticide? Surprisingly, it may also be of benefit to the females, because it synchronises their births and that has all sorts of long-term benefits for their cubs, especially their sons. Cubs with lots of companions do much better than those with few age-mates. They are more likely to survive to maturity, and once they start reproducing they have more young. But there may be even more to the males' behaviour. Although they don't hunt for the cubs or look after them, they do at least protect them, and by keeping away other males they prevent their own cubs being killed. The lion could simply fertilise the lioness and then be off, but that would not be successful. Abandoning your partner is only a good idea for a male if there is a reasonable chance that she can raise the offspring success-fully, and lions probably could not.[38]

Where fertilisation takes place outside the female's body, as it does in many fishes, the roles may sometimes be reversed. The female lays first, and makes her escape while the male is shedding his milt over the eggs. She can thus turn the tables and leave him holding the babies.[39] Single-parent families in which the male takes care of the offspring are indeed much more common among fish than other animal groups. The male stickleback, for example, builds a nest of weeds and plant debris in the middle of his territory. Much of his courtship consists of enticing the female to lay eggs in his nest. Once she has done so he fertilises them and chases her away. He alone then cares for the eggs, fanning them to keep them supplied with oxygen and making sure that the young fry don't stray out of his territory, in which they are safe from many predators.

It is often the case that neither parent does much in the way of caring for the young. The female produces the eggs and endows them with a supply of nutrients. The male fertilisers them. One or both may select a safe place to leave the developing young, but they both abandon them. This kind of behaviour is almost unknown among birds and mammals, but it does crop up elsewhere in the animal kingdom. Most fishes abandon their eggs, and so do many frogs and turtles. Unprotected young are going to suffer much heavier losses than ones being cared for by a parent, and so evolution has selected individuals that lay vast numbers. The codfish, with its ten million eggs in a lifetime, is a prime example.

Organisms, during evolution, must decide between caring for offspring and abandoning them. We can be sure that natural selection will favour those types that leave more successors than their competitors, and very often that will mean that both parents must make an effort. The option of desertion does not exist. If a male, say, were to abandon his mate she might not be able to rear any offspring at all, whereas if he stays to help they will both be successful. This is overwhelmingly the common pattern in birds, probably because bird offspring are so demanding. The eggs need to be supplied with food stores, then incubated, and the young must be fed and looked after. Two animals stand a much better chance of doing enough work than one, and it is among the birds that we find most examples of both parents actively caring for the young.

The four strategies for parental behaviour are quite clear. The male may desert the female, as does the ruff, and this seems to be the prevalent pattern in nature. Or the female may desert the male, like the stickleback. Both parents may abandon their young, like the codfish. Or both may stay and co-operate to raise the brood, like so many birds. The behaviour of birds often seems the most seemly to us, perhaps because it is closest to our own pattern. We care for our young, and may think it heartless of some species to abandon fertilised eggs, but this is misguided. The only aim of life is to reproduce. A pair of tits, devoting almost all their waking hours to provisioning their brood, is meeting that aim in one way. A codfish, feeding until she has enough resources for a million eggs, is doing it another way. People represent yet another way of reproducing. There is no right or wrong, but the variety of patterns helps illuminate the central problem.

The different sorts of parental care will allow very different sorts of mating systems to occur. For example, if only one parent is needed to raise the young successfully it will be possible for the other to seek additional mates elsewhere. This is polygamy, and if, as is usual, it is the male who has more than one mate, it is called polygyny. If, as in certain rare but fascinating cases, the female has more than one mate, the system is called polyandry. When both parents are needed to rear the young, the system will be monogamous; the specific pairing may be for life, or it may not last beyond a season or even a single mating. Real life is generally more complicated than our simple categories allow. Many species are polygamous under some circumstances, monogamous under others. (Some, like the human species, may show all three options in different environments, but these are very rare.) Nevertheless, it is possible to discover aspects of an animal's environment that seem to be associated with one type of mating system or another.[40]

Monogamy is the simpler system, so we will consider it first. There are many environmental influences that will tend to favour monogamy. For example, if there is a severe threat from predators, it will pay both parents to look after the young. Between them they may be able to keep a better lookout, or even beat off attackers. Then again, if food for the young is hard to come by, two parents will be needed to cater to the offspring's needs. Sometimes there may be no spare mates available; if all the females are ready to mate at about the same time a male could find that by the time he has mated with one there are no other receptive females remaining. It may then pay him to stay with his mate and help her rear their young.

Despite all these factors, monogamy is rare. It is most common in birds, where more than 95 per cent of known species are monogamous. Most probably this is a reflection of the huge demands that reproduction makes on birds. We have already seen that eggs, which must be stocked and incubated, and young, who need plenty of food to grow, can stretch even two birds to the limit. Some species overcome the difficulties of caring for young simply by sharing all the duties. The female herring gull, for example, nurtures the egg, but during this time the male will often bring her an extra titbit to eat, perhaps ensuring that she has enough to devote to the eggs. Both birds build the nest, such as it is, and they take turns to incubate the eggs. When the young hatch the parents continue this turn taking, so that while one is out fishing or scavenging on the local garbage dump, the other is at home protecting the nestlings.

Not all birds, however, share parental duties in this way. African hornbills divide the labour. The female builds a nest in a hollow tree and once she has started to lay the male incarcerates her with a wall of mud across the entrance hole. He leaves a small gap, and while she is incubating hunts for both of them, passing food to her through the hole. This continues after the young have hatched, with the male supplying food to the female, who in turn gives it to the nestlings. Eventually there is no room in the hole for the female and her young. With the male's help she breaks out of her cell, but the pair then wall the young up again, for their own protection. Male and female now share the business of bringing food to the young and finally break down the wall to allow the young to fledge. This kind of division of labour between the sexes is quite common among monogamous species.

The work of raising a nest full of young is very arduous. Some parents get assistance from earlier broods. The Florida scrub jay, for example, often hangs around its parents' nest and helps them raise a subsequent clutch.[41] This is a puzzle. How would a bird be selected to forego its own breeding and stay as a helper at the nest? The answer is that it is helping close relatives, who are likely themselves to be helpers. The choice for a young Florida scrub jay is clear. Either it goes off to breed on its own, with all the risks that that entails, or it stays home to help its parents produce more brothers and sisters for it. Assume the benefits of staying outweigh the costs of not breeding, else we would not see helpers at the nest. (It may be that this is not the case; the parents might be able to manipulate the young into staying, and the strategy is actually maladaptive for the young.) Mostly, those benefits come in the form of additional brothers and sisters, enabled to survive by the extra food, and perhaps protection, provided by the helpers. Those extra brothers and sisters probably carry the genetic propensity to help at the nest, and so helping can become widespread in the population. Helping behaviour ensures the spread of the genes that cause helping behaviour and there is no need to look any further for an explanation of why this behaviour should be selected by evolution. A gene that ensures its own reproduction is a success. There may also be direct benefits to the helpers. Perhaps there is not enough space for all to nest, and a bird that helps its parents may inherit their territory when they die. It will also learn its way around the territory, and in all likelihood become much better at gathering food as a result of a season's practice. But these are very likely secondary benefits.

(69)

The business of practice is, however, very important for mono-gamous species. If successful reproduction requires two mates to co-operate, one can imagine that they will get better at it as they learn one another's peculiarities. This is indeed the case in kitti-wakes.[42] Birds that have been together for a few years make better (that is more successful) parents than ones that have just paired. It isn't just a matter of age and experience; if one bird should die, the other will often find a new partner, but the new pair is rather like a pair that has not nested before, so it seems that kittiwakes have to learn to work with each other. When a clutch fails, for whatever reason, the pair is much more likely to break up afterwards. Each may then find another mate. (Some people regard this as a form of polygamy, but it isn't really, because the number of mates is, on average, the same for each sex.)

Monogamous systems represent a way for the female to get some extra investment out of the male. Indeed, in a perfect monogamous system the two sexes will each put exactly the same amount of effort directly into rearing the young, and unless they can reduce their parental investment there will be no incentive to either sex to seek additional matings. For that reason, the differences between the genders are very small in monogamous species, and it can be very hard to tell them apart. Blue-footed boobies share their parental duties as a lifelong monogamous pair, and they are all but impos-sible for us to distinguish. The female has a slightly larger dark centre to her eye, but that is almost the only visible difference between the sexes. The female still produces a few large gametes, and the male many small ones, but in order to ensure the survival of their joint offspring male and female have, as far as looks and behaviour are concerned, become almost asexual parents. They both carry out the same parental duties and both have been tailored by selection into a form fitted for those duties.

Since females are apparently limited in their reproductive success by the amount of effort they can channel into their young, one might imagine that they will always benefit by squeezing a little extra direct parental effort out of the males. At one extreme, this will lead to monogamy. But the ways in which females coax that extra investment out of males are many and varied and will be considered later in this chapter.

Polygamy is altogether more common in the animal world than

monogamy. This is not surprising, as males evolved to compete for female favours. Some will undoubtedly be better at that competition than others and they will get more matings. If there is an equal number of males and females (and there are good reasons to expect this to be the case, see Chapter Five) then some males will perforce get no matings, while others get more than one. The number of matings enjoyed by the most successful males gives some measure of the degree of polygyny. The elephant seal is an extreme example. Burney LeBoeuf and his team from Santa Cruz have been studying the seals of Ano Nuevo Island for many years now. In one season, they watched as 5 of the 115 males performed 123 of the 144 copulations. In other words, 4 per cent of the males accounted for almost 90 per cent of the matings.[43] The species is highly polygynous. In the wren, most males have but a single partner, though some do manage to attract a second or even a third. So the wren is mildly polygynous, not nearly as much as the elephant seal.

The degree of polygyny will have a profound influence on what Charles Darwin called sexual selection. This is natural selection acting on any character that enables an animal to mate more successfully. Males that have to compete with one another may do well to be large and muscular. The elephant seal is three times the size of the female as a result of this intrasexual selection. Weapons too can be selected for the edge they give a male in fights with other males. This is not the only explanation of weapons; male and female reindeer both have antlers, perhaps because they use them against predators such as wolves rather than, or in addition to, fights with one another. In many antelope the female too has horns, but a thorough analysis has shown that whereas the male horns are adapted for clashes with other males, the females' are more suited to stabbing predators. Sexual selection can also operate between the sexes, usually as a result of the female choosing some particular male characteristic. This is called intersexual selection, and the peacock's tail is a good example. Peacocks do not display at one another; each uses his tail to excite the peahen. If the female prefers males with a larger tail, then intersexual selection will increase the average size of a male's tail. The genes that make for a large tail ensure their own success because females prefer large tails. (Sexual selection will be considered in more detail later, when we look at choice.)

Polygamy is favoured from the start by the differences between males and females, but we can still ask what kinds of conditions will make it especially likely.[44] One of these is obviously the richness of the environment. If it is easy for one parent to see to the needs of the young, the other will be free to devote its energies to finding further mates. Among birds, there are two types of nestling. Altricial species hatch blind and helpless; they need a great deal of feeding and looking after and usually this requires both parents in a monogamous mating system. Precocial species hatch at a much more advanced stage, and can walk about and feed themselves; one parent will generally suffice. Not surprisingly, then, polygyny is much more common among precocial birds such as the chicken and pheasant than among altricial birds like songbirds. But even in altricial species, there are some that are polygynous. We have already mentioned the wren, and there are others too.

The important thing in these cases is the quality of a male's territory. If the male has managed to garner an especially rich supply of food it will be quite easy for one parent to feed the young without help. Imagine a female faced with a choice between two males. One is unmated and available to help with parental duties, but has a very meagre supply of food on his territory. The other is already mated, but has a very rich territory. She might well do better to be the second mate, working alone on a good territory, rather than the only mate on a poor territory. And where territory quality varies widely, as it does in marshland, polygyny is much more common than where territories are all much the same. Only 14 of the 291 North American songbirds are polygynous, and 8 of those nest or feed in marshes. As there are only 18 species that nest or feed in marshes among the 291, polygyny is clearly much more common (in fact about 20 times more common) in marshes than elsewhere.

Polygamy generally requires the members of one sex to exercise control over some resource or other. That way, he can take advantage of the females who gather to use that resource. The orange-rumped honeyguide is another excellent example.[45] Beeswax is an essential part of the honeyguide's diet, which means it has to seek out bees. (Man has learned to take advantage of the bird to guide him to honey.) In the breeding season males fight for control of the airspace around a beehive. These are few and far between, so all the females in a given area have to come to the local hive sooner or later.

When they do, the male is able to mate with them. At one hive, a single male mated with 18 females during the season, so clearly it pays a male to gain control of a hive. If there were more hives, so that few females came to each one, it wouldn't be worth the male's while to defend them. The costs of keeping other males away would not be matched by the benefits of extra matings.

Resource defence is usually not as simple as the honeyguide and its wax. Territory in general is a resource, but the specific commodity that is important to the female varies from species to species. Some male territories provide food. This is the case with many birds, and as we've seen it may pay the female to be the polygynous mate of a rich territory holder. Others provide protection, like the male stickleback who keeps other sticklebacks, which would eat the eggs and young, away from the nest. Male impala defend a patch of savannah against other males. The females wander freely from one male's territory to the next, and while they are on a territory the owner has the opportunity to mate with them. The better the grazing on his patch, the longer the females are likely to stay and the more matings a male will get. Red deer stags operate a very similar system. They defend a patch of grazing on which the hinds accumulate. Such polygynous systems are often described as harems, but that is perhaps misleading as it suggests that the male has ownership of the females as such. He does not. He owns some resource, and it is the resource that attracts the females.

Pinnipeds—seals, sea lions and walruses—are a closely related group of carnivorous mammals that have returned to the sea, but not yet as completely as whales have. The females have to come out of the water to give birth, and the way in which they do so illuminates the relationship between resources and polygyny. Good rookeries, which are easy to get to and protected from predators, are quite rare, so that seal cows from a large expanse of ocean crowd on to quite a small area of coastline. The females thus clump together by virtue of their shared need for a safe place to whelp, but once clumped they are an irresistible prize for competitive males. The outcome is the massive male elephant seal and his domineering tactics.

But not all seals show the huge discrepancy between male and female that we expect of a highly polygynous species. Nor do all seals congregate into crowded rookeries. Those that haul out on to pack ice, for example, have more than enough space to spread out. And the seals that give birth on pack ice tend to be monogamous; no male could afford to exclude others from an area big enough to contain more than a single female. Confirmation of this story comes from those species that use land *and* ice. Crabeater seals sometimes breed on pack ice and sometimes on land or fast ice. (Fast ice is ice that is attached to land; it is effectively an extension of the coastline, with few spots suitable for hauling out of the water.) When they are on pack ice the females are very scattered and there is no sign of polygyny. When they are on land or fast ice the females clump together and thus give the males the chance to compete for access to many females. Polygyny is rife.

Resources thus often hold the key to mating systems. Mating systems, in their turn, help us to understand the biology of the animals we are looking at. In particular the difference between the most successful and least successful males—the degree of polygyny—has a profound influence on the difference between males and females and the particular attributes of the male. This is because the degree of polygyny directly affects the strength of sexual selection. We have already mentioned this briefly, and will have to deal with it again when we come to consider the choice of a partner, but this is a good time to look at one species with this approach in mind.

Red deer once roamed all over Britain. Now they are confined to isolated areas, especially in Scotland. One such area is the island of Rhum, one of the Inner Hebrides. The Nature Conservancy acquired Rhum back in 1957 and the whole island, which is about eight miles square, is now a nature reserve, on which scientists have studied the plants, rocks and animals. Of the animals, the most famous are the red deer, the subject of years of research by Tim Clutton-Brock and his colleagues from Cambridge. It is a long haul from Cambridge up to Mallaig, and then across on the boat to Rhum, but the many journeys made by the dedicated team of researchers have given us a clearer picture of the life of the red deer than of almost any other animal.[46]

Clutton-Brock knows all about every one of the deer that roam the four bare hills of Rhum. He knows when they were born, who their parents are, how successful they have been in the struggle to leave offspring, and a whole host of other minutiae. We are concerned especially with what he has learned about the stags.

As in elephant seals, stags are bigger than hinds. But the difference, though impressive, is not nearly as great. The bull elephant seal is three or four times the size of a cow, while a good stag is only half as big again. And, not surprisingly, the degree of polygyny in red deer is lower than in elephant seals. In addition to mere bulk, the stag also has his antlers, which the hinds do not. These he uses in fights against other males. The antlers can inflict a very nasty wound on an opponent, and stags have been blinded by a fortuitously well-placed point. But that is only in the last resort. The stags first try to settle their differences without fighting.

The owner of a patch of land has rights over any females that may gather there during the rutting season. But he is constantly challenged by bachelor stags. A contest begins with a bellowing session. The stags roar out their challenge across the hillsides. Usually, that is all there is to it. The challenger roars to announce his presence. The owner roars back, and the challenger leaves. Clutton-Brock showed that the faster a stag could roar, the stronger it was. Roaring is a very tiring business, and the stags must put an awful lot of energy into it. So only a fit and healthy stag can roar four or five times a minute. By playing tape-recorded roars at different rates, Clutton-Brock established that the stags use the speed of roaring as a measure of fighting ability. If the owner roars faster than the challenger, the contest stops there and then. So sexual selection through competition between the males has led to the evolution of an honest signalling system—a stag in poor condition simply cannot roar—and that helps each stag avoid fights he cannot win.

If the roaring of the two stags is closely matched, the fight enters the second round. The stags walk alongside one another in a so-called parallel display. One gets the distinct impression that they are sizing one another up, and especially looking over their opponent's weapons. Again, most fights do not continue further. But for the few that do, the next stage is the most dangerous. The stags face one another and lock antlers. This is where the points come into their own, for they prevent the antlers getting close enough to do injury. With antlers locked, the stags push one another backwards and forwards, each trying to gain the advantage. This, rather like an arm-wrestling match between two people, is a test of strength. But strength is not the only consideration. Skill counts for more, and the old and wise stag who stands on high ground to bear down on his challenger may win many a fight against a younger and stronger challenger.

Fighting is also much more dangerous than arm wrestling. Stags frequently get hurt. They lose an eye, or pull a tendon, or even break a leg. With winter coming on, even a mild injury can be deadly, and stags do die as a consequence of losing a fight. No wonder that there are two preliminary stages of assessment, in which the challenger especially can see whether the risks he undoubtedly faces are outweighed by his chances of success and the size of the prize. This is no empty ritual to prevent members of the species damaging themselves unnecessarily, as has been thought. It is vital self-preservation, for the stag that runs to fight another day may win more in the end than one who rashly enters combat with a stronger opponent.

Even the winner does not do all that well. The effort involved in being a successful harem owner is enormous. The stag has to prevent the hinds from straying, keep an eye out for youthful challengers, deal with them, and all the while tries to gather more females himself. This leaves him literally without time to eat. The stag's massive neck contains reserves of fat, but the work of harem master may still leave him too exhausted to survive the winter. What does he have to show for an effort that may cost him his life?

The typical harem contains a score or so of hinds. A rich enough prize, except that half of them are probably immature and unable to breed. And one-third of the calves are unlikely to survive their first winter. So in a single season a stag may father no more than five or six calves that live to see their first birthday. Nor can he keep this up for long. Only rarely is a stag successful for more than four or five years. The top stag on Rhum so far fathered twenty-five offspring in his lifetime. Not that great a performance compared to, say, an elephant seal. But many stags are completely unsuccessful, and because of that evolution is entirely on the side of the stag who is a little stronger, has a little more cunning, a little more stamina. The result is a red deer stag designed, by natural selection, to do one thing well: compete for mates.

No such pressures fall on the hind. She needs to bear calves, true, but need not starve while rutting, nor fight other females. So the hind is smaller than the stag, does not have his fat reserves, and does not have his rack of points. Mating system moulds the sexes; where the sexes have similar roles they will look similar, but where each can pursue a different route to success each will be adapted to take that route.

Resources thus hold the key to mating systems, and mating systems to behaviour. But there are also examples in which a polygynous mating system does not seem to depend on the male being able to offer the female anything that she needs, other than his genes. One that we have already dealt with is the lek. The males compete for rights to a piece of space, and females choose the males who occupy the prime properties, but there is nothing much to distinguish one male's territory from another's, except for the females' preference. Because there are far more males than receptive females at the lek at any one time, the females' preference for particular places will mean that the males on those places will get more than their fair share of matings. On one lek of nineteen male ruffs, the three most popular males cornered more than half of the females.[47] Leks are not restricted to birds; they are quite common and have been described in species as diverse as antelope and fruitflies.

Another example in which resources seem to be less important is the male dominance hierarchy. Among social animals in general, and primates in particular, the males often arrange themselves into a ladder-like pecking order (so called because the phenomenon was first described in hens, who use aggressive pecks to settle their disputes). Dominance hierarchies have been the subject of acrimonious disputes among experts in animal behaviour. Some people claim that they are the key to all understanding while others deny them any importance and say that they are simply a manifestation of our own preoccupation with questions of class and status. The answer, as usual, probably lies somewhere between these two extremes. Certainly in the case of mating rights it pays to be a high-ranking monkey.

Monkeys and apes use sexual behaviour for all sorts of reasons besides the primary one of reproduction, most notably as part of the social language that helps individuals to live in a group. Mounting, and allowing yourself to be mounted, have thus become signals of dominance and submission, relative power. (Mounting does not necessarily denote superiority; in some species a truly dominant individual signals his or her status by permitting others to mount.)

Because of this, if one looks simply at copulation, one finds that less dominant males do indeed get quite a lot of sexual access to females. But it isn't really sexual, it's social. In one troop of yellow baboons, who live in the savannah of Amboseli National Park in Kenya and have been intensively studied for more than two decades by a group from the University of Chicago, the three most dominant males copulated, on average, once every five hours.[48] Each of the remaining 11 males copulated less often, perhaps once every 20 hours. This fourfold difference suggests mild polygyny. But if one focuses on that day of the female's oestrus cycle on which she is most fertile and thus most likely to conceive, the figures tell a different story. The top three are now mating about once every four hours, and they are keeping the low-ranking males away; the subdominants manage only one copulation every 35 hours or so. The discrepancy between dominants and subordinates has doubled on the day that counts.

Again, as with leks, the dominant male has nothing to offer the female but his genes. Nevertheless, she would be foolish not to choose him, for the very genes that made him dominant will probably help her sons achieve the same status and that in turn will promote the reproduction of their, and her, genes.

Leks and dominance hierarchies lead naturally to the question of mate choice. If a female is going to get nothing but genes from her mate, how should she select the genes that will do her offspring most good? But we must postpone discussion of this until we have dealt with the other side of polygamy, namely polyandry. Species in which a female mates with more than one male are very rare, but they offer great insights into the workings of gender.

The dunnock, or hedge sparrow, often has two males mated to a single female, but this seems to be the result of intense rivalry between the males, each of whom would prefer to be alone with the hen.[49] Large cock dunnocks can hold a breeding territory and exclude other males from it. They will raise a clutch with a monogamous female. Smaller cocks cannot defend a territory at all and will not breed. But middle-sized birds end up with a territory and an interloper; one bird is clearly dominant over the other, but cannot actually exclude him. The female thus has two males on one breeding territory. The alpha male spends a lot of his time trying to keep the beta away from the female, but he is not entirely successful, not least because the female will actively seek out the beta male and solicit copulations from him. Neither male seems too keen on this, and as part of their courtship they peck at the female's cloaca until she discharges a small pale gelatinous mass. Nick Davies, the Cambridge zoologist who uncovered the private life of the dunnock, watched this happen and then searched patiently on the ground for one of these blobs. He discovered that it was made up of sperms, which the female is saving to fertilise the eggs when they are ready. Presumably each male is trying to ensure that he alone is the father of the clutch, but the female confuses the issue by laying a single clutch in one nest. If both cocks have copulated with the female then, despite their attempts to get rid of the rival's sperm, each will assume parental responsibilities and bring food for the nestlings. As a result the young grow faster and survive better than nestlings supplied by a single father. So there is conflict between the sexes; the female will do best if she can persuade both males that each has a stake in the brood (and could do even better if she could control fertilisation so that only the alpha male's sperm got to her eggs), whereas each male would do best to be the sole father.

So the dunnock, while sometimes polyandrous when there is no option for the males, is not really very different from other birds. A complete contrast is the American jacana, a tropical bird rather like a moorhen.[50] The jacana is often called the lilytrotter because it is equipped with enormously long toes that enable it to run over floating vegetation. Jacanas breed all year round, and have been studied in detail on their Costa Rican breeding ponds by zoologist Don Jenni, of the University of Montana. The female defends a large territory on a suitable pond, keeping other females away. Males guard smaller areas within the female's territory, and there is usually more than one male per female. The average is 2.2 males per female, but one female in the study had four males on her territory. This imbalance is not due to any shortage of females, because there are always spare nonbreeding females available to take over any territory that falls vacant. Each male builds a scrappy nest of floating plant matter, and when it is ready he invites the female to lay her eggs in it. This she does for each of her males. The males do all the incubating and look after the precocious chicks.

When Jenni examined the behaviour of the jacana in detail, he found that there had been an almost complete reversal of the normal sex roles. The female is larger and more pugnacious. She defends the territory on which her mates breed, and she supports them in squabbles with other females' males. If it were not for the fact that she produces the large gametes, the eggs, we might be tempted to describe the jacana hen as a male, so completely has she adopted the behaviour we normally associate with males.

The jacana is the only bird known in which the female regularly has more than one mate at the same time. And the bond between a hen and her cocks seems to go beyond merely sharing the space in which they live. She interacts with all her mates continually, not just during copulation, and if one bird should die or be removed it is some time before a replacement will be accepted by the missing bird's mate. Other birds do have polyandrous systems, but all seem to be decidedly more complicated than the relatively simple role reversal of jacanas.

The species that perhaps comes closest to the jacana is the Tasmanian native hen.[51] A female normally has a single mate, but she will sometimes accept two brothers, and very occasionally three or even four males will mate with a single female. The group (which may also include additional adult females) then stays together to incubate and rear a single clutch. The Tasmanian native hen is like the jacana in that the female mates with more than one male at the same time, but in all other respects shows none of the striking sex role reversal we might expect of polyandry. Males do not perform most of the parental duties and so are not a resource to be competed over; females do not court males. The flock, which is composed of birds related to each other, works together to rear one female's offspring; this is essentially like many more common breeding systems, with the small but important difference that the female has mated with more than one male.

Perhaps the most complicated of unusual mating systems is found in birds such as the tinamou and the rhea in South America. They practise both polygyny and polyandry. That seems contradictory, but it works like this. Males compete with one another to gather harems. The hens lay in a male's nest, sometimes leaving him with a total of as many as fifty eggs. They then split up and move on, repeating the whole performance with another male, and perhaps even a third. So the males are practising simultaneous polygyny; each is mating, at the same time, more than one female. And the females are practising successive polyandry; they have one mate at a time, but mate with several males during the breeding season.

A modified version of this strategy has been called rapid multiple clutch polygamy. A female red-legged partridge, for example, will lay two clutches on a male's territory. One is the male's exclusive concern, while she looks after the other. If nothing untoward happens, both clutches will hatch and, because the young are so precocious, the pair may well be able to raise a second and third batch in a single season. If one of the clutches is lost, perhaps to a fox or some other predator, then that bird will leave to seek another partner. The male might attract another female, if he has lost his clutch, or the hen may wander off to another cock's territory if she has lost hers. So both sexes have the opportunity to mate with more than one partner in a single season. The red-legged partridge's system is very unusual, and probably an adaptation to the highly unpredictable environment that they live in and the heavy predation that afflicts birds that nest on the ground. The females are able to convert resources into eggs very quickly; that not only helps them to take advantage of seasons that are better than average, but also allows them to replace eggs lost to predators.

Perhaps the single most interesting thing about mating systems is that they are not random and promiscuous. Animals do not simply copulate with every suitable partner they meet. This is hardly surprising; animals, especially sexual animals, are bound to vary and anything that enabled one animal to select a better than average partner with whom to mate would inevitably spread. The female, being the sex with more to lose from a poor mating, is commonly the more selective sex. But the paradox arises of what there is left to select. Natural selection, by promoting one type at the expense of others, uses up the very variation on which it depends. If females have been choosing the best males for many generations, one might expect that all males will be much the same, so there is little to choose between them and no benefit to be derived from making a choice. This is emphatically not the case, as a very elegant experiment by Edinburgh zoologist Linda Partridge reveals.[52]

Partridge tackled the problem of female choice in fruitflies, for all the usual reasons; they are convenient, easy to work with, and already well understood. Some females mated with a partner that Partridge had selected at random from a large population of males.

Others were allowed to make their own choice from a selection taken from the same population of males. Both females laid roughly the same number of eggs, and roughly the same number survived to adulthood. At that time, the offspring were each pitted against a standard opponent in a test of competitiveness. The females who had been given a choice produced offspring who were much more successful than those mated at random. Whether the result of female choice or competition between males to decide access to the females, Partridge's experiment shows quite clearly that female fruitflies can enhance their reproductive success by choosing their partner. The question now remains of what exactly to choose. (Do we need to say again that when we use such words as 'choose' and 'select' we do not mean to imply that animals go about these procedures in the same way that we might, with rational thought and conscious decisions? But they behave as if they did, and that is enough.)

We have already seen that quite often the male simply controls some resource that the female needs, and she gets the male with the best resources, willy nilly. Usually, of course, he will be a high quality male, simply because he is in control of resources. But if the male is going to help in the business of raising offspring, then the female would do well to select a male who shows conspicuous ability to do just that.

Sometimes the help is indirect. Male African village weaverbirds provide a nest for the female, but don't otherwise offer much parental care. The male builds his nests out of strips of grass and builds as many as he can on his territory. When a female approaches he displays noisily to her, bouncing and flapping as he hangs from the entrance to the nest. This may be a way of demonstrating to her how strong the nest is. Fresh green grass is indeed strong and flexible, but as it dries it becomes brittle and weak. The male tears down old brown nests and builds anew, but the female is not going on colour alone. Brown nests sprayed green are not very attractive to her. The female is choosing a strong nest and probably also a good area, because unless the feeding is easy the male will not have time to build fresh nests very often.

Whatever the male provides, the female will assess. Moorhens show partial role reversal, in that females are bigger and more belligerent than males. Large moorhens conquer smaller ones in fights, and get the pick of the males. The males they pick tend to be smaller than average, a curious choice, but one that makes sense. Male moorhens do most of the incubating, and to do that efficiently they need good food reserves, so that they do not have to keep leaving the eggs to feed. Up to a point, a small male can supply his own needs more easily, which allows him to build up better fat reserves than larger males.[53] When Marion Petrie, who studied these birds on the ponds of East Anglia, examined the smaller males, she found that they were indeed relatively fatter than the larger ones. So for a female moorhen, small and fat is beautiful.

For birds, one of the most important components of parental behaviour, especially for those with altricial young, is feeding. Feeding yourself can be hard enough, but when you have hungry nestlings to supply the job becomes very taxing. That, we've suggested, is one reason why so many birds are monogamous, because it takes two parents to gather enough food for the nestlings. But if a bird is going to enter into a monogamous relationship, it would make sense to find the most efficient provider possible. Many birds go in for a behaviour called courtship feeding; during the early phases of courtship the female behaves for all the world like a juvenile, begging the male for food, which he duly provides. For a long time experts considered this a delightful ritual that served to emphasise the female's dependence on the male and to cement the bond between them. But it makes much more sense in the light of the anticipated demands of the offspring.

Terns dive for fish to feed themselves and their young, and feeding seems to be an important part of courtship, even between long-established pairs. A careful study revealed that the male brings most fish to the female just when the eggs she is producing require most energy.[54] And there is a strong relationship between the amount of fish a male brought during courtship and the weight of the clutch when fledged, which suggests that a good fisherman is a good fisherman whether he is feeding a mate or her young, and that a female tern would be well advised to select the male who brought her the most fish during courtship.

Often, though, the female will derive no assistance from her partner, just his genes. Under these circumstances the males will often fight among themselves for access to the females, and the clear implication is that the winner of the male fight is the best male to mate with, because his sons will inherit his qualities. Once the dominance hierarchy among the males is sorted out, you might think the female can do little about it, but you would be wrong. Take elephant seals. It is not only the beach master who copulates with the females; his closest rivals will get their share of attempts too. But the cow makes an enormous fuss when she is being mated. The effect of this is to draw any males in the vicinity towards her, and she becomes the focus of intense rivalry. The outcome is usually that the most dominant male chases away the others and returns to impregnate the cow. She continues to make a noise, but the subdominants can do little to displace the beach master.[55] By promoting war and offering herself to the victor, the female assures her offspring that their progenitor will be the best available.

Leks operate on similar principles, although the female doesn't incite direct competition between the males. But the presence of a female does cause the males to redouble their display efforts, and this may sway the female's preference from one to another. The lek is a curious phenomenon because it seems to be the outcome of an irrational preference by the females. They prefer certain sites on the lekking ground, but there appears to be absolutely nothing special about those sites. Often they are in the middle of the ground, but they may be at an edge too. The females' preference, irrational as it is, nevertheless sets up an entirely conventional prize that the males can strive for. But what is it that enables a male to achieve success on the lek? Only his location, and he comes to that largely by waiting. Occasionally one of the holders of a preferred territory will die or become too feeble to hang on to his place. When that happens a bird from a neighbouring territory, not quite so preferred, is liable to get in, leaving a still less desirable space available. This reaction passes through the lek until a space is vacant that can be occupied by a young and inexperienced bird. The longer a male lives, the more chance he has of eventually making it to one of the coveted attractive territories. So one thing females are selecting is male longevity, and that is a good idea because it means that if there is any genetic basis to male quality her offspring will live long and be more successful than average. But it isn't enough simply to live long. Animals on the lek do not respect age *per se*, and there are continual tussles. Not only longevity but also vigour in old age will ensure that a male will be successful, and those very qualities are likely to make a female's offspring high quality too. Success breeds success.

Females travelling to a lek in search of the occupant, whoever he may prove to be, of a particular piece of space, bring us to perhaps the most bizarre instance of female choice, so-called runaway sexual selection, which we dealt with briefly when we considered the effects of polygyny. This is no more than fashion, but fashion with an evolutionary basis. Let us suppose that some females, for whatever reason, prefer males with a long tail. That being the case, males with longer tails will be sought after and competed for by females. This kind of preference could start off very subtly. A longer than average tail might be preferred because it made life slightly more difficult for its owner, who was thus probably of slightly better than average quality to have survived. But if the female preference for longer tails is sustained, there will very quickly be selection for longer and longer tails, until the tail itself becomes the object of desire, rather than any good qualities in the male that it may be associated with. There may be many better males around in the population, but without long tails they will not do well in the competition for females. So why doesn't a female simply go against the crowd and mate with a short-tailed male? She would probably gain by doing so, at least in the short term, but her sons would have short tails too, and so would be less attractive to females. In the long run, a female cannot afford to swim against the tide; she must conform to the prevailing fashion, or her offspring will be unfashionable and thus unattractive and unsuccessful.

It was Sir Ronald Fisher who first pointed out that this sort of preference is self-reinforcing.[56] Once most females prefer some characteristic, for whatever reason, the sons of any nonconformist female will be at a disadvantage. And he felt that runaway sexual selection was necessary to account for the more extravagant sexual ornaments, such as the peacock's tail. Fisher's theoretical model seemed plausible enough, but some biologists doubted the importance of runaway sexual selection in real life. The problem is to demonstrate that females really do prefer the male's adornment itself, rather than some other quality of the male that is associated with his ornament. Malte Andersson, a Swedish biologist, has now shown that in at least one case runaway selection really is the most plausible explanation of male extravagance.[57]

Male African widowbirds have very low tail feathers that they display in a slow undulating flight over their breeding territory. It seems that females are attracted to males with longer tails; certainly long-tailed males get more mates in a season. But that could be because long-tailed birds are genuinely superior and able to hold better territories. If that is so, then changing the male's tail should not affect his attractiveness, provided he remains on the same territory. But if runaway sexual selection has been operating, then the females should prefer the longest tail available; the only force keeping tail length down is the harm that accrues to males with very long tails and offsets the benefits gained from their extra attractiveness. Andersson counted the number of females on each male's territory and then shortened the tails of some birds and lengthened the tails of others. To make shorter tails he snipped a section out of the tail feathers and rejoined the tip with superglue. For longer tails, he used the snipped out middlesection and inserted it into normal-length tail feathers. He then saw how many females the doctored males managed to attract over the next month. Males with extra-long tails were even more attractive than males with normal-length tails. The females' preference is clear, and has almost certainly been the main force behind the evolution of the male's extravagantly long tail.

Females, because they have invested more in their egg from the start, have more at stake in a mating. They are thus almost always the choosier sex, whether they are choosing male genes, resources held by the male, or male parental abilities. But there are occasions on which males too are not quite as indiscriminate as we might expect. One factor seems to be pre-eminent in affecting the male's selectivity and that is the likelihood of fathering offspring. A simple example is the North American checkered white butterfly.[58] The males and females are indistinguishable to us; both look white. But the white conceals a pigment that absorbs ultraviolet light, which the butterflies, like many insects, can see. Males carry more of the pigment than females, and so appear darker to one another. This is how the checkered white tells the sexes apart, because males that have been 'bleached' with a chemical that removes the ultraviolet pigment become attractive to other males. But the story isn't that simple, because bleached females are not more attractive, as one might expect if there were a simple relationship between darkness and gender. Males seem to prefer butterflies with intermediate amounts of pigment, not so dark that they are probably other males, but also not too light. The value of this preference, it seems, is that the pigment fades with age, so a lighter female is likely to be older. And an older female is less likely to be a virgin. Her eggs will probably already have been fertilised, so rather than waste time courting an already mated mate, the male chases off after darker, and hence, younger, females.

The male checkered white makes little contribution to the next generation, other than his gametes and the time it takes him to court the female (which may also expose him to predators). Yet still he is selective. Where the male invests in the offspring he is even more likely to be choosy, and where fertilisation takes place inside the female's body he has a very special problem; he cannot be certain that he is the father. This is the problem of paternity certainty (or uncertainty) and most examples of male mate choice can best be interpreted in its light.

The male who invests anything more than his gametes in the next generation has a severe problem to contend with. If fertilisation takes place inside the female's body, an adaptation that has cropped up several times independently because of the protection it offers the developing zygote, then the male has no guarantee that it is his gamete that is going to get the prize. He can inseminate the female right enough, but all of her gametes may already have been fertilised by another male. And in species that need both parents to care for the young, any female unlucky enough to have lost her partner, whether through death or desertion, would do very well to entice another male to be a caregiver, even though not a parent. The unfortunate male is then in the position of investing in another male's offspring. In anthropomorphic terms, we can say that the male has been cuckolded by a philanderer. There will be intense selection pressure on the female to cuckold a male if at all possible, and even stronger pressure on males to avoid being cuckolded. Certain tactics adopted by the male seem specifically designed to minimise the chances of him inadvertently increasing a rival's reproductive success.

Perhaps the most straightforward anti-cuckoldry tactic is guarding. So long as she is fertile, the male does not let the female out of his sight if he can help it. That way, he may be able to prevent her succumbing to a rival's attentions. We have already seen that dominant dunnocks do this to the best of their abilities. Still, the female does occasionally evade the alpha male and so there is the further adaptation of pecking at the female's cloaca, which causes her to eject the sperm she has just received.

Swallows expend even more energy guarding their mates.[59] Females lay a clutch of four eggs, one each day. For the three days before laying, and while she is completing the clutch, the male tries not to be more than a few feet from the female at any time. He follows her wherever she goes, and if you sit by a swallow colony you will see pairs jinking together through the air as if tied by an invisible thread. You will also see threesomes, and that is precisely what the male wants to avoid. The interloper is a stray male who will, if he can, force the female to the ground and copulate with her—rape, essentially, although most biologists now prefer to call it forced copulation. As long as the female is fertile and laying, her mate will guard her jealously; as soon as the clutch is complete he leaves to harass and rape any females whose mates are not as attentive. And there you have the male dilemma in a nutshell; all males would like to dupe another male into caring for their young, but no male would like to be duped. So males are philanderers, but expect their mates to reject philanderers.

Starlings pay a particular price for their mate guarding. When the nest has been built and the clutch is being laid, the female often leaves to go and feed. The male accompanies her on the trip. But while they are both away, another female starling may come to the nest and dump one of her eggs in it. The returning pair doesn't recognise the foreign egg, and cares for it as they would their own. So both members of the pair are duped into providing parental care for a rival, a penalty that they could avoid if they took turns to guard the nest. Presumably the risk of cuckoldry to the male outweighs the costs of occasionally being parasitised by another pair.

This might be the way that the cuckoo itself, which also dupes male and female, but of a different species, into caring for the wrong young, got started on its particular road. Other birds closely related to the cuckoo parasitise one another, and it isn't difficult to imagine a proto-cuckoo perhaps making a mistake and depositing an egg in another species' nest. At first there would be nothing to tell the hosts that they had been conned, because very few birds can recognise their own eggs. But those that could reject the cuckoo's egg would be at an enormous advantage. Nowadays cuckoo eggs resemble their hosts' quite closely, which is probably the result of prolonged selection by clever hosts.

The cuckoo gave us the word cuckold, and shows us that the duped bird may alter the parasite's behaviour by selecting, for example, cuckoos that mimic host eggs. It would be nice to know what other species of cuckold might do if the male had some idea that his female had indeed been inseminated by someone else, but there is precious little information on this from the animal world. Lions, as we have seen, despatch their step-children, and part of the reason may be to avoid investing in another male's offspring. David Barash did one study that was at first hailed by the more credulous biologists as an example of a prudent bird.[60] Barash studied mountain bluebirds, and placed a stuffed male bluebird near the nest at three different stages in the reproductive cycle. He then watched to see what the resident male did. If the interloper appeared during incubation or when the eggs had hatched, the male did nothing much. But if he was present during nest-building and laying, Barash said that the male attacked the *female* and drove her off. This divorce reaction would certainly make sense, but alas it seems to be untrue. Later studies found little evidence that the male rejected the female.[61] He did attack the model, but even this might not be anti-cuckoldry behaviour; the male attacked stuffed sparrows near the nest site as vigorously as he attacked the stuffed male bluebird, so perhaps he is just protecting his nest site, which may be a scarce commodity. But the female does distinguish between other bluebirds and sparrows. During nest-building and laying she attacks stuffed female bluebirds violently, but she more or less ignores sparrows. This suggests that she is protecting herself, and her mate, from bluebirds who, like starlings, are trying to dump extra eggs in some dupe's nest.

The male, as we have seen, can be choosy about his mate, particularly when he is going to invest in the offspring. But females have to protect themselves against deserters. Talk is cheap, and the world is full of seducers. A female must ensure that a male she permits to mate with her will provide for her and not do a runner at the first opportunity.

This really is a problem, not just a convenient anthropomorphic analogy. Some birds, it seems, make an informed decision to bring up a brood on their own. This is where the male has a particularly good territory with sufficient food or nest sites for more than one female. The male does not help with second or subsequent mates, who must do all the parenting themselves, but presumably those females know, in an evolutionary sense, what they are letting themselves in for. But there are real deceivers too.[62] A male pied fly-catcher is quite capable of defending two territories, separated in space from one another. He may attract a mate to each. With the first female busy incubating the eggs, he now has the time to spend courting a second female on the second territory and persuade her of his honourable intent. But once she has settled down and laid, he abandons her to raise the brood alone and returns to help his first mate. She has truly been deceived, because there are almost certainly bachelors around and they would make better fathers.

One way to avoid deception is to insist upon a direct contribution from the male. The contribution is generally the straightforward one of food. Hanging-flies are small insects that live in the woods of North America, and the preferred subjects of Randy Thornhill at the University of New Mexico.[63] The male hunts for small insects, but, when he catches one, instead of eating it he simply holds on to it and uses a special scent to advertise for a female. The female finds the male, who offers her his nuptial gift. She takes it, and allows him to copulate. The larger the insect he has caught, the longer it will take her to consume it and the longer he can copulate. This is important because it can take twenty minutes for him to transfer his sperm. (It would be interesting to know why he takes so long to transfer his sperm, but that is beyond the scope of this discussion.) If she finishes her meal before that she will break off the mating and all will have been in vain. But if the male's gift is particularly large, and there is still some left when he has finished inseminating the female, he will snatch it away and start advertising for another mate. The hanging-fly's contribution goes directly to the eggs, and as these are abandoned anyway there is no question of the male deserting. (There are other insects that present the female with an empty gift of a silk balloon, a signal that is thought to have been derived from a nuptial meal, but in this case it is doubtful that the female needs any contribution from the male.)

The male hanging-fly presents the female with a meal and lives to mate again. Other males are not so fortunate. Male spiders and mantids regularly fall prey to the very female they are courting. Indeed, in some species of mantis the male can copulate sufficiently vigorously only if the female bites his head off, otherwise inhibitory nerves in his brain prevent his body from being active enough. And having killed the male, she would be foolish to waste him. So the male makes a very direct contribution to the female's welfare and that of the next generation.

Other payments that the female can extract from the male include prized resources that he is defending, as we have seen. But perhaps the most important commodity is the male's time. The best way to ensure that a male is not playing fast and loose with you is to be slow and coy yourself. Only a male not already committed to another female' will have the time to devote to a prolonged courtship. An additional benefit is that he is unlikely to have the time, in one season, to court more than one female. So there is little to be gained by desertion, and he will do better to stay and help to raise the offspring. This perhaps is the reason why females do sometimes insist on a long courtship before finally allowing the male access to their gametes. But a long courtship can work to the advantage of both parties; it assures the female that the male will be a good parent, and assures the male that he has not been cuckolded by the female.

The ring dove, an elegant member of the pigeon family, provides an example that is now quite well understood.[64] Pigeons are rare among birds in that they have a special adaptation for feeding the young. They produce a sort of milk by sloughing off the cells that line the crop. This pigeons' milk is a highly nutritious food for the squab, and both parents can provide it. The female obviously wants to ensure that her male will remain to provide pigeons' milk for the brood, and the male wants to ensure that if he is going to provide milk for a brood then the brood carries his genes. So there is a long courtship. It takes at least five days of interaction between the pair, and often longer, before the female lays her first egg, and during that time, especially after she has first permitted copulation, the male guards her zealously. That much is understandable. But the male is actually hostile to a female who responds too quickly, attacking her with pecks and blows from his wings. A little thought reveals that this is a sensible move on his part; if it takes five days to get a female ready to lay, then any female who comes on fast must already have experienced courtship from another male. And if she has been courted, she may also have been inseminated. In which case the male might be fooled into providing his valuable milk for another male's offspring. So it does not always pay a male to mate rapidly, at least not if he is going to have to assume parental duties thereafter. Caution and delay can improve his certainty of paternity.

Animals in the wild show a wide variety of mating systems, but there are common threads that link them all. The first is that the sex that offers more in the way of parental care will become a resource for the other sex to compete over. Normally, because of the initial difference in size between egg and sperm, it is males who compete over females; the occasional reversals of this only make us more confident of the basic premise. But females do not simply mate with any old male; they choose those males who have most to offer, whether the offer is resources such as food or safe nest sites, help as parents, or simply good genes. Females can require males to provide more than genes, and a parental contribution from the male may be indispensable. But they must be wary of being deserted by a philanderer.

The female's insistence upon parental care by the male has the effect of making the male choosy, though he is seldom as selective as she, so that he avoids making an investment in offspring that do not carry his genes. This too might seem to be more of a theoretical problem than a practical one, but it is not. In one famous experiment all the male red-winged blackbirds who held territories on a marsh were vasectomised. This prevents them fathering offspring, but does not otherwise alter their behaviour. And yet, even though the territorial males had been vasectomised, fertile eggs appeared in the females' nests.[65] Presumably they had gone elsewhere for their gametes, and as the vasectomy had not interfered with the copulatory ability of the males one must assume that extramural matings are a normal feature of red-winged blackbird life. Red-winged blackbirds are mildly polygynous, and the male does not provide much parental care. Which is just as well, as he runs the risk of caring for unrelated nestlings. It is, alas, a chicken and egg problem; if the male were more certain of paternity he might provide more care, and if he provided more care he might take more trouble to be certain of paternity.

The only goal of life is to reproduce. Sex has given rise to gender, and thus to different ways of going about the business of reproduction, two different sex roles. But there can be no difference between the sexes in the total amount of effort directed into reproduction. Females may put their effort into care while males put theirs into competition, but the total effort must be the same. If it were not, it would pay animals to concentrate on the sex that reproduces cheaply. They do not, and the sexes are inevitably kept in balance.

THE SEXES IN BALANCE

We have been saying that sex is often unnecessary and that males are parasites on females; why then are there any males? Or, a little less harshly, why are there so many males? It is females whose resource gathering matters, which means that females govern the size of future generations, and so we might expect animals to divert most of their effort into female offspring. A few males might be needed to fertilise the females, but most success would come from the females. And yet, almost everywhere we look we find male and female offspring produced in almost equal numbers.

The reason turns out to be stunningly simple, and like so many other such ideas belonged originally to Sir Ronald Fisher.[66] Fisher's argument runs like this. Suppose that in a monogamous species there is indeed an imbalance between the sexes so that there are many more females than males. Suppose also that individuals vary in that some produce more males and others more females. Any individual who does produce more than the average number of males will do better than average; males are in short supply so a greater parental contribution to males will result in more matings and more grandchildren. Those grandchildren will tend themselves to be male, and they will inherit the tendency to produce males; on both counts the proportion of males in the population will go up. As the number of males approaches the number of females the advantage of producing males declines, until at 50:50 the benefits of producing the two sexes are equal.

The beauty of Fisher's reasoning is that it is perfectly symmetrical. Substitute male for female, and vice versa, in the above paragraph and the logic is unchanged. So any deviation from a sex ratio of unity—equal numbers of males and females—will automatically be corrected by this so-called frequency-dependent selection. (The strength of selection depends on the frequency of genes in the population. When there are few males it is very worthwhile producing males, but when males are more frequent the benefit of biasing your offspring to males is much less.)

The mating system being practised has no effect on the outcome of the argument, except in certain rare exceptions that only strengthen the main case (and that we deal with a little later). Imagine, instead of Fisher's monogamous society, the more usual polygynous one. All females mate, but only a few males do so. Let us say that each female produces two offspring in her lifetime. Nine out of ten males are unsuccessful but one is a big winner and fathers 20 as a result of 10 matings. Again, the naïve view would be to produce males, but that would be wrong because although a male will produce ten times more offspring than a female, the chances that he will do so are only one in ten. The extra prize is exactly offset by the longer odds against winning.

The essential point is that every offspring has two parents. Although the total reproductive success of all the males and females in a population is therefore necessarily equal, if the numbers of the two sexes are not equal the average success of a member of the rarer sex is bound to be higher. It doesn't matter that, for example, in humans the male is capable of reproduction for far longer than the female; what counts is that each offspring has two parents. That puts a premium on the rarer sex, which as a result becomes more common.

We have treated Fisher's explanation of sex ratio in terms of numbers, because that is simple. But the idea, as Fisher saw, is more general than that. Equal numbers of male and female offspring is really a special case of equal investment in males and females, and investment is at the bottom of sex ratios. In this context, investment is any effort an organism devotes to one offspring at the expense of future offspring. Such investment will comprise several costs and these may be outweighed by the benefits that accrue. Unlike an economist, the biologist cannot measure costs, benefits and investment in terms of money. The biologist thinks in terms of reproductive success, and may measure this as, say, number of offspring that survive to maturity. But even this is only an approximation to the real currency of evolutionary success, just as money is only an approximation to the elusive concept of utility.

To return to animals, it might be the case, for example, that males are much smaller than females and hence easier to produce. (Again, the logic is symmetrical.) If, say, sons are half as expensive in terms of parental care and so on then it would pay parents to have sons rather than daughters, unless a daughter's prospects for future generations are double those of a son. The female would cost twice as much as the male, but would produce twice the offspring. This will happen, of course, when there are twice as many males as females. But males, we said, are half the cost of females. So at the balance point—two sons to every daughter—the total *costs* of the two sexes are equal. What really matters is not the sex ratio as such but the ratio of parental investment in the two sexes.

This helps us to make sense of occasional puzzling sex ratios in many species, including our own. There are about six boys born for every five girls in human populations, and yet by retirement old women outnumber old men. The reason is the higher mortality of males. At almost every age a girl can expect to live longer than a boy, as we might expect if males have been selected for a competitive existence. What that means is that boys, by dying, deprive their parents of the opportunity to keep investing in them. If equal numbers of males and females were born, then, because males curtail parental investment, total investment in males over the parents' lifetime would be lower than total investment in females. That would be an unstable arrangement, favouring parents that invested more in males. And one way to invest more in males is to have more of them. Some will die young, but over a lifetime investment in males will equal investment in females.

Fisher's explanation is a very clear example of what has become known as an evolutionarily stable strategy, or ESS. An ESS is a strategy that does best against itself in any evolutionary struggle; it is the strategy, in a specified set of alternatives, that cannot be bettered. So, if we imagine three sex ratio strategies—produce predominantly females, produce predominantly males, and produce equal numbers of each—only the last is an ESS. If everyone in the population is producing 50:50 males and females then no other sex ratio can do better.

All this may seem like an overly convoluted explanation for a phenomenon that seems, after all, inevitable. If we have two distinct kinds of sex chromosome called X and Y (or W and Z in birds) then meiosis is automatically going to produce equal numbers of gametes bearing each of the two types. And that in turn means equal numbers of the two genders. So why do we need Fisher's argument?

For two reasons. First, we are entitled to wonder why meiosis should have evolved to produce equal numbers of gametes bearing X and Y chromosomes. (Indeed there are a few very interesting mutations that are lethal when homozygous but survive by biasing gamete production towards the heterogametic sex—that is XY (male) in mammals, ZW (female) in birds. These are called meiotic drive mutants.) ESS theory provides one kind of answer. More importantly, there are species in which the gender of an individual has nothing to do with any specific sex chromosomes. Before we return to some of the ramifications of sex ratios we want to explore other sorts of sex determination.

'The turtle lives 'twixt plated decks, which practically conceal its sex.'[67] So wrote Odgen Nash, but that has not prevented biologists from probing between the decks, and what they have discovered makes a very interesting story. When a female turtle hauls out of the ocean and up the beach she selects a spot on which to dig her nest and lay her eggs. The temperature in the nest is crucial for the development of the eggs, and obviously depends on a whole host of factors, such as sun and shade, winds, tides, and so on, that the turtle can be but dimly aware of. If the eggs are too hot or too cold they will not develop, but provided it is between 26 degrees C and 34 degrees C baby turtles will indeed emerge some time after laying. Because of the plated decks it had always been assumed that the sexes were equally represented in the hatchlings, but that turns out to be untrue. The sex of a turtle depends crucially on temperature during development. At 26 degrees C all the eggs hatch as males; at 34 degrees C, all are female. Equal numbers hatch only if the eggs were at about 30 degrees C.

A female cannot possibly predict the temperature at which her eggs will develop, so she cannot guarantee an even split between the sexes. Perhaps the average temperature, taken over all the nests made each season, is close to the balance point. Or perhaps there is some special reason why turtle sex is so odd. We just don't know. We do, however, know that the turtle's peculiar method of sex determination has important consequences for its survival. Turtles, especially the large marine turtles, are threatened with extinction. To save them, well-meaning conservationists have removed eggs from nests and incubated them in special polystyrene nest boxes. They then raise the hatchlings for a while to give them a head start before releasing them to the ocean. This is thought to be a good idea, because the most severe pressure is on the very young turtles as they make their first mad dash to the sea. As they scurry down the beach they are easy meat for all the predators around, who feast on the baby turtles. Ordinarily that wouldn't matter; enough survived to breed. But with the turtles so threatened, every turtle saved is valuable. Unfortunately, the temperature inside the artificial nest boxes is slightly lower than average, about 28 degrees C. The result—100 per cent males. The very opposite of what conservationists might want.[68] Alerted to this by Nicholas Mrosovsky of the University of Toronto, who studied the sex of headstarted hatchlings, turtle conservationists are now paying much more attention to the temperature in their polystyrene nests.

It is hard to imagine an adaptive reason why sex determination should be handed over to the caprices of weather. And whatever scientists might come up with, it will have to be a robust enough theory to encompass the Mississippi alligator too. The alligator, like the turtle, determines sex by temperature, but in exactly reverse manner. Eggs incubated at low temperatures turn out female and those at higher temperatures are male. The balance point is about 32 degrees C. Mark Ferguson, of Queen's University in Belfast, studied the alligators in the swamps and levees of Louisiana, and discovered that it is the temperature between 20 and 35 days after laying that is most important.[69] The alligators lay in three distinct sorts of locale: up on the levees the ground is dry and the nests warm, resulting in 100 per cent males; nests in wet marsh were cool and hatched exclusively females; and in dry marsh the nest temperature was intermediate, with eggs from the hotter part turning out male and those from the cooler parts turning out female, with an overall ratio of five females to every male. Indeed, five to one was the average sex ratio over all nests in four consecutive years. What this means for the breeding system of the alligator is hard to say. Certainly females were heavier when they hatched than males. This is because development and metabolism are slower at lower temperatures; females thus need less food to develop, and consequently have more left when they hatch. These heavier females mature more quickly than light females and males, so they can start reproducing sooner, and that alone may be the pressure responsible for the evolution of temperature-sensitive sex determination. But it cannot be the explanation for turtles, in which everything is reversed.

Sex that depends on temperature is no mere quirk either. It may be behind the very reason we are here today. The mammals that eventually gave rise to ourselves had been around a very long time before they expanded and radiated into their present dominant status. While the dinosaurs ruled the Earth the mammals remained tiny creatures of the undergrowth, and only when the dinosaurs died out were the mammals free to occupy the niches vacated by the extinct reptiles. There have been many hypotheses to account for the death of the dinosaurs, several of which invoke a change of temperature. Usually this is said to affect food plants, or the dinosaurs' ability to keep warm (or cool). But if dinosaurs, like turtles and alligators, relied on temperature to decide their sex, then they might have gone extinct because one sex was no longer produced.

Temperature is not the only unusual factor to influence sex. Presence of other animals can be very important. There is a marine worm, called *Bonellia viridis*, that lives in a burrow and extends an enormously elongated proboscis to feed. The worm is about 8 centimetres long, but the proboscis can be ten times longer, up to 80 centimetres, and sweeps around on the mud picking up bits of food. At least, that is how a female *Bonellia* manages. The male is just 5 millimetres long, and lives as a parasite inside the female's womb. He is little more than a source of gametes, the ultimate male function. *Bonellia* larvae are sexually indeterminate—they can grow either way. When the time comes for them to metamorphose into adults, they settle on the seabed. If the larva comes into contact with a female's proboscis, it is affected by a hormone secreted by the female. It enters the female's body and settles down, becoming a tiny sperm factory within about three weeks. If it does not encounter a female, the larva stays put and starts developing into a female, a process that takes about two years.[70] So *Bonellia* cuts its sexual coat very much according to its cloth; if there is a female to take advantage of, the larva becomes a male and takes advantage of her, but otherwise it becomes a female.

Bonellia shows how it can pay an organism to be male in some circumstances, female in others. There are many other species that do likewise. Some fish start life as females within a male's harem.

When the male dies, the dominant female changes into a male, sometimes within a matter of hours. But there is yet another option, that of hermaphroditism, combining male and female in a single body. Fish that change sex are said to be sequentially hermaphroditic. Animals like snails are male and female at the same time. They are simultaneously hermaphroditic. (Hermaphroditus, in Greek legend, was the son of Hermes and Aphrodite. Salmacis, a nymph, fell in love with him and prayed that they might be united as one flesh. Her prayer was answered, and Salmacis and Hermaphroditus became one bisexual body, the male portion of which gives us our name for organisms that are both male and female.)

Hermaphroditism is a very complex issue that has not really been satisfactorily resolved. There are many reasons why it might pay an animal to be bisexual. Perhaps the best one is rarity. If members of your species are very thin on the ground then you double your chances of a successful mating if you are bisexual. (Being bisexual, as Woody Allen is said to have pointed out, doubles your chances of getting a date on Saturday night.)[71] But if that is true, why not go the whole way and abandon sex to become a self-fertilising hermaphrodite? Many organisms have. And why then do we find bisexuality the rule among such plentiful species as slugs and snails? In any case, there remain the problems of male and female; even if we unite them in one body females are nurturant and males exploitative.

A lovely example of this is the black hamlet, a simultaneously hermaphroditic fish that lives in coral reefs in the Caribbean.[72] Just a few years ago, Eric Fischer, while working for his doctorate at the University of California in Berkeley, spent many hours underwater watching black hamlets, and noticed that both genders partake in each mating. But instead of one partner releasing a load of eggs to be fertilised by the other, which would open the door to exploitation of the 'female' function by the 'male', there is a stately exchange. One partner releases a few eggs. It then waits for these to be fertilised, and for the other partner to part with a few eggs. The first animal fertilises these, and then releases a few more eggs. So the exchange goes on, with each animal playing male and female alternately, thereby ensuring that neither is exploited by the other.

To gonochorists like ourselves (that is, organisms in which the two genders are housed in separate bodies) the hermaphrodite has a

peculiar fascination. It seems to offer the possibility of truly understanding what the other gender is like. Martin Daly and Margo
Wilson, as so often, put the matter well when they write: 'The
female-male phenomonon has inspired wistful thinkers, from the
ancient Greeks to the present, to dream of an androgyne who could
bridge the gap and fully experience both sexual identities. Alas, we
mammals are thoroughgoing gonochorists, and communication
between men and women will surely remain imperfect.'[73] But as
we have seen in the black hamlet, male and female functions remain
at odds even when housed in the same body. Bisexuality, interesting though it undoubtedly is, has taken us on a detour from our
main theme of sex ratios and sex determination, to which we must
now return.

One of the most interesting sorts of sex determination is found in
many insects. Females are normal diploid individuals, with a
double set of chromosomes, but males are haploid. Females thus
have direct control over the sex of their offspring. After mating,
they store sperm in a special receptacle called the spermatheca, and
they can then either release some sperm to fertilise a passing egg,
which will make it a female, or leave the haploid egg unfertilised,
which makes it a male. This system, called haplodiploidy, makes
evolutionary sense of the selfless behaviour of social insects such as
bees, wasps and ants, the Hymenoptera.

The vast swarming colonies of ants are composed largely of
female workers. These are sterile, and lay no eggs. Their sole job is
to tend the reproductive queen ant at the centre of the colony. So
too with bees and wasps, the sterile female workers tend the queen
and her offspring selflessly, abandoning their own reproduction and
even dying in defence of the hive. This was a puzzle to Charles
Darwin, who could not see how such altruism had evolved. It was a
problem, he thought, best left to future generations. And it was
solved in the early 1960s by William Hamilton, then a young
graduate student at Imperial College in London.

Hamilton looked closely at the genetical consequences of haplodiploidy, and in particular at the relationships between the various generations.[74] Firstly, there is the relationship between a
queen and her daughters. These contain one of the queen's two sets
of genes, and so there is a 50 per cent chance that any gene of a queen
is also present in one of her daughters. Their relatedness is 1/2. The

same is true of the queen's relatedness to her sons. Although they contain but a haploid set of chromosomes, these are chosen at random from the queen's diploid set. Again, there is a 50 per cent chance of a gene being present in queen and drone. So a queen is equally related to her sons and her daughters. For the workers, things are not so simple. If a worker were to breed, she would be related to her offspring by a half. But consider her relationship to her sisters. Half of their genes come from the mother, half from the father. But whereas the maternal half could be either of the queen's diploid set, all the paternal genes in all the sisters are identical because the drone was haploid and had only a single set of genes to pass on. So as far as their paternal relationships are concerned, all females are identical twins. But for their maternal genes, they are simply sisters, related by a half. The relatedness of two sisters is therefore the average of their maternal relatedness—a half—and their paternal relatedness—one. In other words, workers are related to one another by three-quarters. *They are more closely related to each other than to their own daughters.* And that is why it pays them, in evolutionary terms, to help their mother produce reproductive sisters rather than reproduce themselves. A gene that favours sisters does half as well again as one that favours daughters.

The imbalance in relatedness that occurs because of haplodiploid sex determination is obviously a very powerful stimulus to social behaviour. Societies like that of the honeybee have arisen independently 12 times among the insects. Of that dozen, fully 11 have haplodiploid sex determination. Only one, the termites, has the more usual form of diploidy. If you are more closely related to your sisters than to your daughters, it will be easy for selection to favour genes that channel your efforts to those sisters and their reproduction rather than direct to your own offspring.

But precisely because of the imbalance in relatedness there is also an imbalance in the sex ratio that suits the workers and the queen. The queen is equally related to her sons and her daughters. She should, as a good Fisherian, want to produce equal numbers of males and females. But the workers are three times more closely related to their sisters than to their brothers. So the best sex ratio for them is three sisters to every brother. The queen is in control of producing the eggs, so one might think that she controls the sex ratio. But she hands the eggs over to the workers for 'parental' care, and so they might be able to direct investment in the two sexes to their own benefit. There is a conflict between the generations.[75]

Robert Trivers and Hope Hare looked at investment in the two sexes by measuring the dry weight of male and female reproductives in a number of ant species. (Dry weight was deemed to be the most convenient measure of investment.) They discovered that females were three times heavier than males, a result that implies that workers do indeed control investment in the sexes. But in slave-making ants, which steal larvae from other species and raise them as workers who then tend the brood, males and females were equally heavy. Slaves have no genetic interest in the future reproduction of their masters (though why they continue to act as slaves remains a mystery) and so the queen's will wins out. Perhaps slave-making is an adaptation to favour queens in the power struggle. Other species, such as the wasp *Polistes*, show an investment ratio close to unity, so it is by no means inevitable that workers, despite having to care for the offspring, have control over investment.[76]

Hymenopteran insects, with their ability to control the sex of the offspring directly by fertilising the egg or not, bring us to the question of adaptive control of sex ratios, that is, species in which sex ratio is changed to suit conditions. The Fisherian argument is based on large populations and random matings, and under those conditions it works perfectly. But there are conditions in which equal investment in the two sexes would not be adaptive, and Hymenopterans exemplify most of those. One that doesn't normally apply to other species is local mate competition. Investing in males is valuable because they will have to compete for matings. But what if there is no competition? Some species of mite, *Acarophenax tribolii* for example, reproduce in a seemingly bizarre manner. The female produces eggs which develop into larvae within her body. They reach sexual maturity and the males fertilise the females, who then eat their mother from within. The females emerge, already fertilised, to be devoured in turn by their own daughters. Clearly such a mite has nothing to gain from extra sons, since they will only compete for matings with their brothers. That is the essence of local mate competition; where the competition is largely between brothers there is no gain to be had by producing many competitors and the effort should go into females. The best idea is to produce just one son, who will fertilise all your daughters (although it might be prudent to make a couple in case of accidents), and that indeed is what these mites do. Their sex ratio is highly biased towards females. The principle applies generally, and Hamilton discovered sixteen families of Arthropod in which there was regular brother-sister mating and a bias towards females through haplodiploid sex determination.[77]

Selection for biased sex ratios when there is local mate competition is not that hard to envisage. We can imagine those individuals that produced more females and fewer males outcompeting all others, and so the sex ratio might become part of the genetic make-up of the species. But there are species in which the degree of competition between males is going to vary, and then the female must make an altogether more intelligent calculation.

Nasonia vitripennis is a tiny wasp that parasitises fly pupae. These can be few and far between, so when a female finds one she lays a batch of eggs that contains just a few males. The males develop more quickly than their sisters and emerge from the parasitised pupa first. There they wait for their sisters to appear. The males mate each female as she emerges, and she then flies off in search of fresh hosts. Sometimes, a female will find herself on a pupa that has already been parasitised. What should she do? Obviously she should produce more sons than if she were the only one to lay on the pupa, because her sons will now have to compete for matings against the first female's sons. Indeed there are lots of stimuli that will cause a female to withhold sperm from more of her eggs. And that, because of the peculiarities of haplodiploid sex determination, increases the proportion of males. If she meets another wasp walking about on the pupa, or finds the little hole left by a previous wasp's ovipositor[78] or even if there are lots of female wasps around in the neighbourhood[79] the female will lay more male eggs.

Actually, the female superparasite (that is, one parasitising an already parasitised pupa) has a whole range of strategies open to her, and the sex ratio depends on which one she adopts. If she lays just a single egg it should obviously be a male; he will compete with the first female's sons and probably gain quite a few matings. But if she lays several eggs, the value of additional sons decreases, because they begin to compete with one another. When the number of eggs matches, more or less, the number laid by the first female the proportions of males in the two broods should be more or less the same too. And that is exactly what John Werren, who studied the details of sex ratio in *Nasonia*, discovered.[80]

Local mate competition is one factor that moves animals away from a straightforward Fisherian sex ratio. Another is the effect that increased investment will have on the success of the different sexes. This seems to be the most important factor in mammals, although local mate competition matters too. Galagos, small nocturnal primates of the West African forests, for example, produce more males than females. Females do not move as far from their parents as males, and so sisters are likely to compete for food. That local competition between females may be why galagos produce fewer daughters than sons. But in general it is the differential effect of investment on fitness of the two sexes that biases sex ratios in mammals and insects.

To deal with insects first, it is clear that the haplodiploid system offers enormous power to the mother to make the best investment possible. (Father, of course, would prefer all daughters as he has no stake at all in sons.) Among solitary bees and wasps, for example, the female does all the work of gathering food for her offspring. Being big is often better in such circumstances. Bigger females live longer and lay more eggs. They can collect more food to provision those eggs, and may have an edge in fighting other females for access to prime nest sites. For males, who compete largely by scrambling for females, rather than by fighting, size probably does not contribute too much to breeding success. So if there were lots of food about, mothers would do well to produce females who can take advantage of the food to grow big and be successful. Not surprisingly, that is exactly what they do.

Sweat bees provision brood cells with a little ball of pollen, moistened with nectar. The queen lays an egg on the food source. If the pollen ball is large, she fertilises the egg and it develops into a female. If it small, she lays a haploid egg which is male.[81] If the mother is a parasite, then the size of the host may dictate the sex of the egg, larger hosts receiving female eggs. *Lariophagus distinguendus* is a tiny wasp that lays a single egg inside a weevil larva. The weevil is itself parasitising a grain of wheat. If the weevil larva is small, less than 0.6 mm, then the wasp lays an unfertilised male egg. But if it is 1.1 mm long the proportion of males falls to just one in five. So the wasp adjusts its sex ratio to make best use of the available food. It is actually even cleverer than that, because it seems to keep track of the relative abundance of different sized weevil larvae. Eric Charnov's group at Salt Lake City offered *Lariophagus* females weevils 1.4 mm long in three different ways. Some females got a succession of 1.4 mm larvae; they laid 15 per cent male eggs. Other wasps were offered 1.4 mm larvae and 1.8 mm larvae alternately; they laid 30 per cent males in the 1.4 mm hosts. A third group received 1.4 mm larvae in alternation with 1.0 mm larvae; they laid just 2 per cent male eggs in the 1.4 mm hosts.[82] So the female matches her sex ratio not to the absolute resources of the host but to the relative size of each larva she finds, putting males in the smaller ones and females in the bigger.

Mother-eating mites and smart wasps are all very well—indeed to a biologist they are particularly good because they are easy to study—but they don't arouse much empathy in us. We want to know about animals closer to ourselves. How do they cope with the investment split between males and females? The problem, of course, is that because of chromosomal sex determination birds and mammals do not have the same degree of control over the sex of their offspring. But there are options open to them, such as directing investment to one sex or the other as soon as they can distinguish the two. The result is a hotch-potch of examples, some of which clearly support all we have been saying about sex ratios while others are more contentious.

The field has been very ably reviewed by Tim Clutton-Brock, whose own research on red deer has done so much to illuminate parental investment and sexual strategies.[83] Perhaps the first thing to get out of the way is the fact that mammals can and do bias sex ratios, despite the constraints of meiosis. Opposition to the idea has come largely from agriculture, where a bull that could sire predominantly females would be invaluable to the dairy industry. An analysis of more than 150,000 calves from 107 bulls revealed almost no variation among the sires in the sex ratio of their progeny. But in other species the outlook is not so gloomy. Several mammals, including our own species, do bias sex ratio towards males, particularly at birth. We have already seen that this may well be a response to the competitiveness and hence increased mortality of males. There are two species of lemming, however, that routinely produce an excess of females. This is probably because some females have an X Y pair of sex chromosomes that include a mutant X that somehow makes the bearer female and biases the production of eggs in favour of itself. But why an excess of females should be favoured in these species we do not know.

Very often there is a relationship between the sex ratio at birth and the delay between ovulation and insemination. What seems to be happening is that Y-bearing sperm are more vigorous, but also more vulnerable, than X-bearing sperm. (We are tempted to speculate that this is the earliest manifestation in his life history of the male's competitiveness and the mortality it brings.) So if insemination takes place long before fertilisation, the Y-bearing sperm die off and predominantly X-bearing sperm remain; they will produce female offspring. If insemination is close to ovulation the increased vigour of Y-bearing sperm gives them an edge and males result. The interesting thing is that the simplest predictor of the delay between insemination and ovulation is the frequency of intercourse. If intercourse takes place often, there is a good chance that it will occur close to ovulation. If it is less frequent, there is likely to be a delay and the X-bearing sperm will have the advantage.

It is said that the proportion of boys born goes up after wars. This may do something to restore the balance and replace the young men lost, but would it be presumptuous to suggest that the mechanism might have something to do with an increased frequency of copulation? And on a similar note, despite all the pre-birth speculation, we were not at all surprised that the first offspring of Prince Charles and his lovely bride was a boy.

So sex ratio is not always fixed at unity. Nor, indeed, is it necessarily fixed at any particular value. Laboratory mice normally produce a 50:50 sex ratio, but when they are kept on a low-fat diet the proportion of males drops to just 24 per cent. White-tailed deer show the reverse effect. They normally produce 47 males to 53 females, but when they are deprived of food the ratio changes to 70:30. In fact many ungulates seem to produce more males when the population density is high.

Perhaps the strangest example of variable ratio comes from some work done at the University of Indiana. Nancy Burley, like practically everyone else who studies birds, used colour rings to identify the zebra finches she was working on. She noticed that some colours were more attractive than others. For example, a black ring contrasting against the orange leg of a male made him much more attractive than, say, a blue ring. When she came to look at the sex of the clutches, Burley discovered that they seemed to be biased in favour of the more attractive sex. Hens mated to an attractive cock produced more males, while if the hen was the more attractive of the two the clutch was biased towards females. There have been many objections to Burley's work, some of which she has met, and it is too early to say whether this very strange phenomenon is genuine. If it is, it will mean a great deal of rethinking in the ornithological community. And it does make sense to us.

Among primates there are some very curious examples of variable sex ratio. Two studies of baboons and macaques have shown that sex ratio is intimately linked to social status. Socially dominant mothers tend to produce an excess of females, while subordinates favour sons. High ranking females among the baboons of Amboseli produced 10 males to 19 females, that is, 39 per cent males. Low ranking females in the same troops produced 68 per cent males. The captive rhesus monkeys of Madingley, outside Cambridge, show exactly the same effect. High ranking females produce 31 per cent males, low and medium ones 61 per cent males. So sex ratio is variable. The vital question is whether the variability has any adaptive significance, and here the evidence is a lot shakier.

Theoretically, we can see when it would pay parents to bias their investment in favour of sons or daughters. Two things need to be true. First, there needs to be a difference in the variance of reproductive success between the two sexes. That is, the most successful members of one sex must be able to do better in the breeding stakes than the most successful members of the other. This, as we have seen, is likely to be true, and generally it will be the males who have the highs and lows of success. Second, parental investment in an already good member of one sex has to improve its chances of being among the highs. Ideally, then, if you have resources to spare, you should invest them in the sex that will benefit more from a little extra. That is what the sweat bees were doing, laying female eggs on large pollen balls. What about mammals?

The laboratory mice obviously fit the bill. Males have the greater variance in reproductive success, but when supplies are low mothers divert what scarce resources they have to females. How they do this we do not know. They may be able selectively to abort male embryos. But white-tailed deer do just the reverse, biasing offspring in favour of males when they are starved of food. And another rodent, the Florida packrat, behaves in the same way as the white-tailed deer. The deer mouse has a litter that is roughly equally divided between males and females. But if times are hard the female actively excludes male pups from her nipples and the nest, and so the sex ratio at maturity is biased in favour of females. And those dominant monkeys who produce daughters are presumably getting more nutrition than subordinates and ought to be channelling it into males.

These exceptions could, of course, not be anomalies at all. It may be that in some species although the male has the greater variance in reproductive success, the female nevertheless benefits more from a little extra. Unfortunately we just do not have the information to tell. It may be the case in baboons and rhesus monkeys because female offspring inherit their mother's rank in the hierarchy. So a mother may be able to influence a daughter's success more than a son's. (But then a bigger, stronger son would surely be at an advantage when competing against others for high status in his new troop.) Alternatively, the biased sex ratio could be the consequence, without adaptive significance, of some other behaviour that is adaptive. In baboons the females all stay in the troop they were born in, while the males leave. One way for any animal to improve its success is to remove competitors, in this case other females. And there is evidence that dominant female baboons direct far more aggression to juvenile females than to males. This harassment extends even to unborn fetuses. Mothers carrying a male fetus are less likely to be attacked than those carrying a female. Perhaps this makes it more likely that a female fetus will be aborted or miscarried, and hence lead to the male-biased sex ratio.

Control of sex ratio in mammals is thus a field ripe for study. We know that some species do it, but we don't know how or why. There are good theoretical reasons why it would be adaptive to vary sex ratio, but as yet no conclusive evidence on the point. Mechanisms too are only vaguely understood. Timing of intercourse is one possibility. The mother may be able to discriminate against sperm bearing one or other of the sex chromosomes. Or she might abort fetuses. Later still, she can channel resources into one sex and not the other. What then are we to make of the one species that has both the means and the motive to adjust sex ratio as it sees fit?

Recently there has been a spate of reports from China that the authorities there are very worried by the increase in infanticide.[84] The figures speak for themselves. In one rural area near the central China city of Wuhan a survey revealed that, among the under fives, there were 503 boys to every 100 girls. In some places the ratio is even higher, 8 to 1. There can be only one explanation: parents are killing their baby daughters (an ancient Chinese practice, though Eskimos do it too and many other peoples did it in the past). This is almost certainly a response to the Government's decree that couples may have just one child. People want a son, and are prepared to kill a daughter in the hope that they will be luckier next time. (Just why they want a son is not clear; one newspaper said simply that young couples cling to 'feudalistic thinking' that favours men over women. The anthropologist Marvin Harris makes a very convincing case that female infanticide is part of warlike behaviour. It enhances the value of males while at the same time keeping the population down. Women thus become a scarce resource, given as rewards to the most important warriors. This can hardly be true in modern China, but it was certainly the case for much of the history of the Chinese people.) Things are bad enough among the under fives to worry the authorities, but they will be much worse when those excess boys become men in search of brides. Then those families who kept their daughters will find themselves blessed with a host of suitors. Sir Ronald Fisher will have been vindicated again.

SEX AND SOCIETY

Although the sexes are, by and large, in balance, they behave in very different ways to achieve the same goal, of maximising their genetic investment in the next generation. As we have seen, because of the fundamental difference between eggs and sperm it is generally males who chase after females, rather than the other way round. It doesn't matter what species we are dealing with, the ideas remain the same. That applies to humans too, of course, but there is an additional element to be considered. We are cultural animals. The details of the culture may vary, but every human being lives within a society. Nevertheless, the rules that govern society are not arbitrary, and many of the peculiarities of human behaviour can best be interpreted as manifestations of the conflict between male and female roles. In this chapter we are going to look specifically at some of the more cultural aspects of human life, while in the next we focus on the more biological side of things.

In many species, males die young as a result of the fierce competition created by the urgent biological imperative to find and mate with as many females as possible. The human animal is no exception. We have already mentioned the difference between men and women in life expectancy; contrary to what they might like to think, men are more vulnerable at all ages. Interestingly, the difference is greatest between the ages of 20 and 30, when a man is more than three times likelier to die than a woman. And this difference is due almost exclusively to what demographers call external causes: accidents, suicides, homicides and poisonings rather than the internal causes of disease and decay. Between 20 and 30 the risk of death due to internal causes is about equal in men and women, but men are five times more likely to die of external causes. Later on in life, after about 55, the two causes become equal, but even then men are still about twice as likely to die as women.

These figures are taken from the 1976 census of Canada, but everywhere the figures tell the same story: men are more vulnerable than women. Margo Wilson and Martin Daly have gone further and analysed sex differences in just one category of life (and death)—car driving.[85] In the United States in each year there are about eight deaths of 16- to 20-year-olds for every million miles driven. Six of the eight are male. For the next half decade, 21–25, there are six deaths, and five of the six are male. Thereafter the number of deaths comes down, but at every age more male drivers are killed than female.[86] Males drive more than females, but these figures take that into account because they are deaths per million miles driven by each sex. What they show is that males drive more riskily, more competitively. Male bravado certainly predates the motor car, but it is interesting to see how this modern phenomenon continues to reflect the male search for power, prestige, and hence evolutionary fitness.

Driving a car dangerously is perhaps risk taking with no great likelihood of payoff, our evolutionary heritage leading us astray in the modern world. Burglary, however, clearly has it uses. In the United States in 1980, 93 per cent of burglaries and 94 per cent of robberies were committed by men.[87] The same pattern is true in almost every culture. Men are not likely to be poorer than women, quite the reverse, but they seem readier to appropriate another's property, and to use violence to do so. Male competitiveness could easily be at the bottom of this striving for goods. Young human males are pugnacious, and do take risks. In that respect they are no different from the young males of many species. In the animal world, it is relatively easy to see how and why 'males are usually the more competitive sex and why they are concerned to maximise matings, while females are not'.[88] Our own patterns of behaviour may appear, at first sight, more complex, more subtle, and less easily explained in terms of the biological imperatives dictated by the roles of large, stay-put egg and tiny, wandering sperm. We seem fundamentally different from other species of animal, but this comforting appearance is no more than a façade. Cultures vary, but beneath them all is the biology of the uniquely cultural human animal. You can think of all sorts of reasons why young men might be more competitive and more willing to take risks, but in the end you come down to our evolutionary heritage, our animal past as it is so often derogatorily called. None of the differences make much sense except in the light of the fundamental biological differences between male and female.

When we look at basics the criterion of success must still be the ability to pass your genes on to the next generation, and to ensure that your offspring survive to breed in their turn. How can this success be achieved by men and by women, given that they start out with very different biological investments in their offspring? An understanding of the problems, and their evolutionary solutions, provides insight not just into normal human reproductive behaviour, but also into patterns of behaviour that do not conform to the norm.

The human male, like the males of other species, is faced by a dilemma regarding his sexual activity. He would like, genetically speaking, to impregnate as many females as possible and leave them to get on with the business of rearing his children. But he cannot be sure that a single mating will impregnate the female; often one copulation does leave the female pregnant but equally, as many couples will testify, it can take repeated attempts over many months. Nor can a man be sure that a woman left holding his baby will be either able or willing to raise the child until it is independent. And while he is out impregnating other women, like-minded men may well be doing the same to him. Parenthood is a monstrous source of confusion. The mother always knows; her mate can never be certain.

An interesting sideline on this is the question of resemblance between baby and parents. People are much more likely to comment on the similar looks—real or imagined—of a baby and its putative father than on the resemblance between mother and child, which is obvious. And the mother, apparently, is the worst offender, reassuring her husband that the child does resemble him.[89]

One way round the confusion is some sort of institutionalised arrangement that gives a man and woman certain formal rights, obligations, and duties. Marriage may be almost impossible to define, but it is nevertheless a feature of every human society. At one time the mechanics, as well as the institution, of marriage were seen as uniquely human; groups of men generally transferred women among themselves. In most other animals, including most primates, it is the males who move between groups of females. But it seems that in our closest relatives, the chimpanzee and the gorilla, females transfer to males, rather than the other way round. So we share our mating pattern with our closest relatives, which means that the pattern itself may well predate the emergence of the human line.

Marriage can be seen as an exchange between man and woman; the man offers parental investment in exchange for the woman's fidelity. But even in marriage, *Homo sapiens* shows its evolutionary origins. One survey of 849 human cultures revealed that only 137 were monogamous. Polygyny, habitual or occasional, was the rule in 708, while polyandry was permitted in only four.[90] It isn't easy keeping multiple wives; they are liable to fight and a man must be able to provide for all of his wives and their offspring; but the gains, if he can afford it, are enormous. Mormon church leaders of the nineteenth century, who had to provide a separate establishment for each wife, averaged 5 wives and 25 children. Lesser mortals, not members of the church hierarchy, could afford only 2.4 wives and fathered an average of 15 children. And the unfortunates who could keep but a single wife fathered just 6.6 children.[91] (Note that the wives of the church fathers did not do as well as those in a mono-gamous marriage; polygyny doesn't usually pay the woman.)

The only way that a man can be certain that a woman's children are also his children is to keep her away from other men at all times. Rich and powerful men have always been able to afford the dual luxuries of a vast harem and the offspring that such an investment will produce. The Emperors of old China are reputed to have copulated with their concubines in strict rotation, such that each was impregnated at the time in her menstrual cycle most favourable for conception. The whole process was overseen by women atten-dants (to prevent cheating) and was probably enormously produc-tive. A thousand offspring is not impossible, and as one anthropologist commented, it 'shows what could be achieved with a well-organised bureaucracy'.[92] One thousand children is a possibility, though the world record for fatherhood is generally ascribed to the last Sharifian Emperor of Morocco. 'Moulay Ismail (1672–1727), known as "The Bloodthirsty", was reputed to have fathered a total of 548 sons and 340 daughters.'[93] But this level of polygyny, possible only with enormous wealth and power, is prob-ably not consistent with our evolutionary past. Indeed, even the Mormons are not typical of most cultures. Polygyny at that level depends on the presence of agriculture to enable the accumulation of great wealth by a few. Among the !Kung-san of the Kalahari, foragers whose way of life has probably changed very little from that of early man, almost all have just one wife. Fewer than 5 per cent have two, and none more. The pattern in our past was probably like that: a single wife for the majority, with the possibility of a second for the most successful.

Polyandry, by contrast, is the rule in very few human cultures, and there are two distinct sorts. The African version of polyandry is concentrated largely in Nigeria, and on close examination is probably more polygynous than polyandrous. A woman may be married to several husbands, each in a different clan. She lives with one husband at a time, and it is possible that she will never go to live with some of her husbands. The marriages are really alliances of power, and as the men too have multiple wives, with whom they live simultaneously, it is likely that even though the wives have many husbands the top men do better than the top women.

The other main centre of polyandry is in the Himalayas and elsewhere in the north of the Indian sub-continent. Among the Tibetans, it seems that polyandry is a device to fool the taxman. Families marry all the brothers to just one wife, whose children inherit all the family holdings. This is preferable to splitting up the family's land and with the Tibetan system of taxes prevents the loss of more land than is absolutely necessary. The brothers who share a wife are not always keen on the idea, but they see it as the lesser of two evils: having to share a wife is bad, but splitting up the family's land is worse. But in the short term, they are probably wrong. One study revealed that a woman with one husband produced more children during her lifetime than one in a polyandrous marriage. Neither men nor women profit genetically from the arrangement.[94] Of course, that short-term comparison of number of children must be set against possible, but unknown, gains that would accrue because the family holdings are not continually divided between sons.

The Pahari of Northern India have quite another approach to polyandry. Here bride-price is very high, so that a group of brothers must pool their resources to afford a single wife. They buy one, and share her, but as soon as they can afford another they do so. And another, and another. The result is a group marriage, so-called polygynandry, in which all the men and all the women share each other. In distinction to the Tibetans, who think that monogamy would be preferable if it didn't divide the family land, group marriage is both what the Pahari get and what they say they want.

The few cases of polyandry can all be understood in terms of specific aspects of the environment that make a shift to this system desirable. The rarity of polyandry indicates, to us, that human beings do seem to have evolved in the context of mild polygyny. But marriage, unlike polygamy, is a universal feature of every human culture. Why?

One answer is that marriage is a way for men to assure themselves of mates. Having a wife, however, does not remove the male's evolutionary inclination to extend his sexual activity as far as possible. And so in the vast majority of cases, even where monogamy is backed by the law, there are opportunities of extra mates for the men. As far as passing on their genes is concerned, there are definite advantages for males in keeping their females to themselves but taking any opportunity to mate with other females. A man wants his own wives to be constant, but he himself would like to be unfaithful with another man's wife. This puts him in a cruel bind, if he wants to promulgate rules about how a wife should behave. The result, a rule and a double standard. Thus a cuckold is an almost universal object of scorn, because he has been duped into wasting his resources on another man's child. But the cuckold-maker is admired for beating the system. So men keep their wives under control, and traditionally do not want their wives to be too easily aroused, but are easily aroused themselves in order to be able to take advantage of another man's woman while his back is turned. Statistics on the use of pornography, and physiological response, bear this out. Men use pornography, and are quickly aroused. Women do not use pornography, and are generally slower in becoming ready, or indeed willing, to have intercourse.

Men, it is said, are polygamous, women monogamous. Statements like this, and indeed many others that we will be making, have been derided as bald assertions, convenient myths with no foundation in truth. That, to put it bluntly, is simply not the case. The evidence of our biological heritage is there for all to see, although of course it does not compel us in any way to do anything. We are masters of our own fate. But the facts remain true. To get back to the male sexual appetite, it is indeed true that men are keener on variety than women are. In one survey of middle-class, middle-aged American couples, 20 per cent of the men said they had engaged in extramarital sex. Only 10 per cent of the women had. Nor is the difference restricted to what men and women say they actually do; it applies also to what they would like to do. Forty-eight per cent of the men, but only 5 per cent of the women, said they would take advantage of an opportunity for extramarital sex in the future if one presented itself.[95] And as in America, so in the rest of the world. Forty-six per cent of young German working-class men, but only 6 per cent of the women, say they would avail themselves of an opportunity for extramarital sex.[96] Even on the kibbutzim of Israel, where one would think that the ready access to medical and contraceptive advice, combined with the supposed ideology of equality, would have some effect on cultural stereotypes, the sex difference remains. More than 40 per cent of adolescent boys, but fewer than 10 per cent of the girls, regard casual sex as 'legitimate'.[97] Surveys of pre-technological people are not very common, but the reports of anthropologists investigating cultures around the world reflect the same discrepancy over and over again, so much so that the pioneering sex investigator Alfred Kinsey concluded: 'Among all peoples, everywhere in the world, it is understood that the male is more likely than the female to desire sexual relations with a wide variety of partners.'[98]

With the advent of computer dating schemes, it has become possible to go beyond what people say they find attractive in a partner to what actually seems to matter, and this has revealed a lovely sexual difference. For one computer dating service, people were rated by means of a questionnaire to measure their 'adherence to traditional religious values' and their 'permissive attitudes toward violation of traditional sexual standards'. Pairs were then created in which the partners were either like one another on these scales or unlike one another. Three hundred pairs were arranged, but only 239 actually dated and were kind enough to send the computer firm an assessment of how the date went. Men found most attractive those women who shared their sexual attitudes; identity of religious feelings was not important to them. But women were attracted to men who shared their religious values, and sex was less important to them.[99] Is it too far-fetched to use this as evidence that men date primarily for sexual reasons, while women are looking for a long-term mate to provide for a family?

Marriage is a device to beget children; almost universally a man can divorce a wife who is barren. He may also be able to claim back some of the bride-price he paid for her. This holds despite the fact that it may be the husband who is at fault. Men do not accept male infertility. And the laws of divorce and adultery generally favour the idea that women in marriage are a man's property. It is the marital status of a woman that counts, not that of her seducer. If she is married, the husband has a genuine grievance and may divorce her. If she is unmarried the seducer is likely to suffer only at the hands of her brothers, or father, whose property he has defiled. But the marital status of the seducer is irrelevant.

Not surprisingly, perhaps, there are specific signals for marital status in different cultures. Bobbi Low, of the University of Michigan, surveyed 138 different cultures as part of a thesis on ornamentation in the human species.[100] Her findings make fascinating reading, but of particular interest to us is the signalling of marital status. Of the 138 societies, 99 have a signal that advertises whether a woman is married or not. But only four of the 138 have similar signals for men. In our own society, practically all married women signal their status with a ring; few men do so. A man can easily tell whether a woman is married, but a woman can be easily deceived.

In pre-technological tribes codified law distinguishes between male and female roles quite clearly; it is the married woman who is guilty of adultery, not the married man. Western law seems more egalitarian in this respect, treating men and women as equals, but this is a recent innovation. Male infidelity was not criminalised in the west until 1810, when the French revolutionaries went so far as to make it illegal for a man to keep a concubine in the marital home *if* the wife objected. And even today, a jealous rage by the husband, perhaps the most common motive for murder, is looked on leniently by the courts. The reason is clear. A man, by his infidelity alone, does no great harm to his wives. A woman may land her husband with a cuckoo in the nest. Or, as the French revolutionaries explained, 'It is not adultery *per se* that the law punishes, but only the possible introduction of alien children into the family and even the uncertainty that adultery creates in this regard. Adultery by the husband has no such consequences.'[101]

Adultery is the most common reason for divorce. Kinsey reported that 51 per cent of divorced American men did so because their wives had been unfaithful. Just 27 per cent of women used those grounds for divorce.[102] The difference is even more striking if you recall that men are actually twice as likely to have indulged in extramarital sex.

If marriage is an institution for the raising of children, what should each sex look for in a partner? A woman shouldn't really mind who fathers her child, so long as its future—which in our society means its economic future—is assured. She wants a husband who can take care of her and her children, but whether he is the father of those children or not they each carry 50 per cent of her genes. The rich man's wife may be entirely happy to cuckold her husband, as long as she is not caught. Equally, of course, no wife should be too worried about her husband's philanderings, as long as he continues to provide for her and her children—what she is worried about is the prospect of some other woman seducing him away from her and leaving her children poorly provided for. Scandal and opprobrium that prevent him from doing his job may nevertheless affect the wife, even if he stays with her.

Here is another sex difference. Women ought to be jealous only if their man invests heavily in another woman. Men should be jealous of sexual liaisons between their wife and other men. Again, that is precisely the difference that turns up in surveys. One enterprising candidate for a PhD at the University of Connecticut got undergraduate couples to participate in a role-playing game that was designed to foster feelings of jealousy.[103] The men turned out to be worried by the prospect of their girlfriend having sexual contact with another man, the women by the possible loss of their boyfriend's time and attention. Even in the matter of jealousies our past shows through.

In base biological terms, a man takes a wife as a reproduction machine, so he wants a fertile woman who will assure him of many children. In quite a few cultures the most desirable woman is one from a large family with many brothers, in the expectation that she will inherit the desirable qualities of fertility and a propensity to bear sons. One way to get as many children as possible out of a woman is to start quickly, and young brides are valued for that reason. Young brides are also more likely to be virgins, something still valued even in decadent western society. This wish was highlighted recently by the 'marriage of the century' between the Prince of Wales and Lady Diana Spencer. The bride was acceptable to the royal establishment in the UK, and presented to an adoring public as the ideal choice by the media, as much because of her youth and apparent lack of sexual experience as because of her personality, pedigree and the fact that she was the one Prince Charles had chosen. Young wives should also be strong enough to bear children successfully, and the Princess of Wales soon lived up to the expectations of the masses in that regard.

So a man should look for a young, healthy and fertile wife if he is to maximise his success in passing on genes to the next generation. What choice of husband should a woman make? We did say that it shouldn't matter to a woman who fathers her children, but this is not strictly true. She looks for two qualities, long life and success. In the animal world, a successful male may be big and strong, able to keep a large harem like the elephant seal or red deer, and his females will bear strong, successful offspring in their turn. In our world, success today may depend as much on intelligence, or cunning, as on physical strength, and it is measured, by and large, in terms of economic power. Whether or not her offspring are likely to inherit the abilities that made their father a success, an economically strong—rich—father will surely give them a good start in life, while long life, if inherited, will give them more opportunities to provide their mother with grandchildren. And, of course, these two qualities are often found in the same man, because it takes time to amass wealth. Wealthy men are often old men, and just a few generations ago only successful men survived to reach old age. Perhaps that is why women find grey hair distinguished in a man, and why premature greyness, a sign of longevity, is so attractive atop a young body. It really is true that a good evolutionary strategy is for beautiful young women to marry rich older men. But perhaps the best possible husband would be the son of a wealthy man, provided he is assured of an inheritance, who will be around to protect his wife and children for longer. This is as true of the Trobriand Islanders as it is of the people of Manhattan; women are far more concerned with a husband's ability to provide for her and her children than with his attractions or otherwise as a lover. It seems that both Prince Charles and Lady Diana made exactly the right choice of spouse, the choice that, given the chance, our own genes would make for us. We somehow recognise this and that is why their alliance strikes such a chord worldwide.

Prince Charles will undoubtedly invest handsomely in little William and his siblings. After all, ours is a supposedly monogamous society and Charles can hardly doubt that he is the father of Diana's son. But if promiscuity is rife, if men are forever philandering with other men's wives, it is a good bet that their wives too have been importuned. If cuckoos are plentiful, the odds are that you have been cuckolded. We've seen that parental investment only makes genetic sense if the offspring who receive the investment are your relations, so what should a man whose wife may well have been unfaithful do?

This question is bound up with the whole thorny issue of kinship and lineage. This is a topic that has occupied anthropologists for decades, and no doubt will continue to exercise them for years to come. For our purposes, we want to consider just two relationships, uncles and cousins. Uncles are very important characters in most societies; your mother's brother may be the soul of solicitude, or he may sell you into slavery, but either way he is a central figure. And this too makes sense. Recall that a husband is bound to be uncertain of his paternity, while a mother knows that her children are hers. That means that siblings are always related, even if they have different fathers, through their mother. If fatherhood is certain, then a man will always be more closely related to his own children than to his sister's. After all, they share half his genes, while his nieces and nephews have half of their mother's genes, which she in turn shares half with her brother. So nieces and nephews are related to their uncle by just a quarter, while his own children are related to him by a half. He can of course benefit if he looks after his nieces and nephews, but he should prefer his own children. So much for straightforward faithful marriage. When mating is more promiscuous, husbands have a much harder time deciding who to invest in. Simple calculations reveal that when the certainty of paternity is less than .268, that is when the chance that your wife's child is also your own is less than about one in four, you are more closely related to your sister's children than to your wife's. So, if you are being wise, you should invest in nieces and nephews, not in your own wife's children. (Your wife's brother should take care of them.)

John Hartung at Harvard looked at patterns of inheritance in 22 different cultures. He put the cultures into four categories depending on whether the level of female promiscuity was high or low and whether a man's heirs were 'his' children or his sister's children. Eleven of the cultures had high female promiscuity, and hence high paternity uncertainty. In six of them the man's sister's son inherited, and in the other five his own son. The other 11 cultures had low promiscuity, and hence low paternity uncertainty. In only one of these did the sister's son inherit, the other ten gave property to their own sons.[104] So in this respect it looks as if an advanced form of human behaviour, namely the passing on of material goods to future generations, follows rules that make biological sense. It is hard to come up with any other feature that all these cultures have in common and that distinguishes the different forms of inheritance as effectively.

So much for uncles. Now for cousins. If paternity certainty is high, then all cousins will be equal. That statement does not make much sense, probably because in our own culture paternity certainty *is* high, and cousins *are* equal. But plenty of cultures make a distinction between what are called parallel cousins and cross cousins. Parallel cousins are related through parents of the same sex; in other words, the offspring of two sisters are parallel cousins. Cross cousins' parents are of different sex; brother and sister are aunt and uncle to a set of cross cousins. When paternity is certain, as we said, all cousins are equal. But when it isn't, cross cousins are probably more closely related than parallel cousins. (A moment's thought will show why.)

We have had to use lots of words to explain a concept that is essentially alien to us, but an Iroquois indian would know exactly what we were talking about. Iroquois, like many people, have words to distinguish the two types of cousin and behave differently towards them. But many cultures, like our own, do not. The link ought to be paternity, and it is. Penelope Greene, also at Harvard, did the same exercise as John Hartung, putting cultures into compartments according to whether they distinguished cross from parallel cousins and whether they were very promiscuous or not. Of seven cultures that did not distinguish cousins, only one was promiscuous and the other six were not. By contrast, of 13 that did separate cross from parallel cousins, 9 were highly promiscuous.[105]

The question of promiscuity and paternity certainty also relates to inbreeding, for if there is a chance that offspring do not share a father then there is less harm to be had from incest. Highly promiscuous cultures do tend to permit closer marriages than less promiscuous ones, but this effect, though suggestive, is weak. We should also bear in mind that promiscuity does not inevitably mean paternity uncertainty, although there are disturbing suggestions that even the most monogamous of societies have their share of cuckoos in the nest. Geoffrey Ashton conducted a mammoth survey of 1748 families, including 2839 children, on the island of Hawaii.[106] He was interested in patterns of inheritance and used a set of 15 biochemical markers to identify the blood and saliva of every subject. These biochemical markers are rather like the familiar ABO blood groups, but more varied. As in legal paternity cases, it is never possible to be certain that someone *is* a child's father, though it is possible to exclude a potential sire. Ashton, with his 15 biochemical markers, was surprised to discover that more than 2 per cent of the children were not the offspring of their mother's husband. That, to a mathematical modeller who might be interested in the evolution of traits in a human population, is quite a high proportion. It further stresses what we have been saying all along, that to understand many aspects of human culture we must understand evolution.

The evidence of past evolutionary pressures is thus clearly visible to the trained eye, and we hope we have convinced you that biology is very important in understanding the elements of normal human society. But evolutionary thinking can also be used to provide fresh insights into aspects of sexual behaviour that are still surrounded by taboos in our own and almost every other human society. We are referring to the unnatural sexual practices, such as incest and homosexuality, that may be more openly discussed today, but are still by and large very poorly understood by most of the people involved in the discussion.

Let's start with incest. There are incest taboos in our own and every other human society. But is it 'natural' to avoid incest, and if so, why? What are the pressures of natural selection that tend to make us choose mates who are not close relatives, and how do they work?

The first thing to make clear is that there is no simple biological reason why incest is a bad thing. It is true that any small group of animals that is suddenly restricted to matings only between closely related partners suffers immediate bad consequences in the form of an increased proportion of offspring who are in some way defective, but this inbreeding depression weeds itself out of the population within a few generations. An incestuously breeding population, whether it is made up of mice or humans, does not necessarily either die out or reduce itself to a collection of mental defectives. The reasons are clear in terms of natural selection and sexual reproduction.

The advantage of sexual reproduction, above all other advantages, is that it provides for variety. If this were no advantage, a female would be better off dispensing with sex and reproducing parthenogenetically, and in a stable environment 'if there were no deleterious effects of inbreeding, a female who mated with her brother would increase her inclusive fitness'[107] by passing on the genes she and her brother share to the next generation. But there are deleterious effects, both short and long term. Every animal that reproduces sexually carries harmful mutations whose effects are masked by the presence of a dominant allele that is not harmful. If related individuals mate, the chance that both of them may carry a particular harmful allele, and therefore the chance that their off-spring will receive two copies of this harmful mutation, without the protective presence of the non-mutated allele, are vastly increased. So if breeding is suddenly restricted to a small, closely related population there will certainly be an immediate upsurge in the number of offspring in which these harmful recessives come into play. This may result in loss of intelligence, or bad eyesight, or sickle-cell anaemia, or any one of a myriad other handicaps in the evolutionary race. But under natural conditions such recessives will be at an enormous disadvantage and would soon be weeded out of the breeding population. It is what happens in subsequent generations that is really interesting.

The survivors will have many genes in common, but there is no reason to suppose that these will be defective. They have survived selection, and so they are adapted and fit, in the Darwinian sense. Provided that defectives are culled from an inbreeding population, the population can survive indefinitely. This is exactly what biologists do to breed up so-called pure strains of experimental animals, like the white mice used in laboratories around the world. Repeated matings between siblings in each generation, and between parent and offspring, have ensured that there are so many alleles in common that the genetic make-up of one Balb/c mouse (to give an example) is exactly like that of any other Balb/c mouse, so that the scientist does not have to worry about genetic differences between his mice and those used in experiments in another laboratory. As a population becomes more inbred, the survivors come to resemble one another more and more closely, so that, in effect, they become clones, genetic replicas of one another.

This is the real price of incest. Like the dandelion or the Amazon molly, the survivors have lost the variability of an outbred sexual population, and while the population may survive indefinitely, it may not be able to adapt quickly enough to a changing environment. A change in the weather, the loss of a food supply, a new predator or even a trivial disease might make scant difference to an outbreeding population but might equally well wipe out an inbred one. In a sense inbreeding animals pay all of the costs of sex but reap none of the benefits. The reasons to avoid incest are no more, and no less, than the reasons why sexual reproduction is, under the right circumstances, a 'good thing'.

We are descended from animals which, clearly, found sexual reproduction an advantage, so it is no surprise to find that we are descended from animals that, by and large, avoided incest and inbreeding. If they hadn't, they might not have been able to cope with the swift environmental changes of our recent past, and they would have left no descendants today. Incest may have been common, perhaps in a community cut off from others, but it has not survived as the predominant human lifestyle because of natural selection. We are the survivors of those members of the human species that had a certain reluctance to mate with their close relatives.

This still leaves the fascinating question of why we should be worried about incest at all, let alone have incest taboos. If we have been selected to avoid mating with near relatives, why does the possibility of such matings ever enter our thoughts? We have little idea why we are conscious of some things and not others, but the answer must surely be related to the fact that we do think, and are not governed by blind instinct and urges. We have created a complex society in which natural selection still operates, but along pathways different from those in the wild. Social evolution is a vast topic outside the scope of this book, but we can outline some of the underlying reasons for the human fascination—even obsession— with incest by following the outline provided (more clearly than anywhere else we know) by Robin Fox, Professor of Anthropology at Rutgers University in New Jersey, in his book *The Red Lamp of Incest*.[108]

It seems likely that, rather than recognising their close genetic relations in some way, most animals treat as a sib all others raised by the same parents, and look further afield for breeding partners. If we look at the human animal in particular, we can see, argues Fox, how the incest taboo might become part of the behaviour pattern of a tribe through childhood frustration. Brothers and sisters, playing together from an early age, become involved in games leading to sexual arousal but offering no hope of sexual fulfilment because their bodies have not yet reached puberty. The result is that siblings become identified in the subconscious as not worth the bother of sexual games. Once puberty has been reached this same subconscious identification with nonsex ensures that individuals outbreed. In psychologists' jargon, siblings are desensitised to one another as sexual objects. This idea is just one of many possible mechanisms that might prevent incest, and it certainly makes sense. But to natural selection it makes no difference how our ancestors avoided incest as long as they did and as long as the tendency to do so was passed on to the increased offspring of those who avoided incest. We can see the same process at work, and causing terrible confusion, in modern society.

Fox points out that where children are brought up together in mixed sex groups and allowed to play freely together they never form mating partnerships with one another when mature. The classic example is provided by the kibbutzim of Israel. Children on many of these collectives are brought up in large nursery groups. They may sleep at home with their parents or in a dormitory, but they spend their waking time together in the group, and most of their activities are done in a group. The cohort of children from different parents behave like an overlarge group of siblings. In more than 20,000 recorded marriages between children raised on the kib- butzim, not a single one has been between a couple who spent the ages from 2 to 6 in the same group. Not one at all, despite some-times intense parental pressure in favour of marriage within the group, and despite the fact that many of the children remain firm friends for life. The children are not genetically related, they like each other, and their parents want them to marry. But they cannot and do not. Some express active regret that this is so; few realise that biology has subverted their culture. The culture offers no taboo, but their biology forbids mating with those whose bodies have become too familiar.

Familiarity, indeed, breeds contempt. But what of the other cliché—does forbidden fruit taste sweeter? Of course it does. In a strict 'Victorian' society, boys and girls are kept apart, constantly chaperoned, and not allowed to join in rough and tumble games together. The result is that brothers and sisters never learn to regard each other as inappropriate objects of sexual desire and just after puberty, or in later life, they may become strongly attracted to one another. This taboo attraction may be heightened in such societies because of the limited opportunities to interact sexually with other people. Fox's argument leads to the conclusion that segregating children by sex at an early age actually causes all the problems that make incest so disturbing to modern society, because it switches off the natural mechanisms that teach us, at an early age, that members of the opposite sex with whom we grow up are not the ones to mate with.

This proposal neatly explains the nature of the incest taboo in human society, and the value of sexual reproduction neatly explains why people in societies that avoid incest, for whatever reasons, are likely to be vigorous and healthy. The problem is that many other species avoid incest, and it is unlikely that the same mechanism works for them too. In most primates, for example, young males leave the troop they were born in when they become sexually mature, and take up residence in another troop. When their time comes to mate, they do not do so with their sisters. In the case of chimpanzees, it is the female that leaves to join a troop of unrelated males, but the effect is the same. Different animals, with different social structures, similarly manage to avoid inbreeding; they simply do not mate with animals that they grew up with, and in the normal course of events animals you grow up with are your close kin. (This is, by the way, a cause of endless bother for zoos trying to breed from their animals.) The actual mechanisms by which this occurs are unknown, but that doesn't matter. Whatever process helps an animal to avoid mating with close kin will, as long as there is a benefit to outbreeding and sexual reproduction, be selected for. Such an animal will do better than one that disregards any prohibition on mating with relatives. The biological mechanisms that make chimps avoid incest may also be present in people, a biological underlay which also prevents the children of the kibbutzim from marrying one another. Under ordinary circumstances culture serves to strengthen the biological imperative.

The mechanisms are less important than the fact that for our immediate ancestors incestuous matings were selected against by evolution. Individuals with a tendency to inbreed were eliminated from the population to some degree, though not exclusively, so it is no surprise to find that today we retain biological evidence of incest avoidance. They exist because they had survival value, but their survival value in present society is very difficult to see, and may no longer exist.

In society today childless 'matings'—and childless marriages—are common, and a couple may stay together for life without reproducing. This may be a failure in Darwinian terms, but it is by no means uncommon. Casual sexual encounters, thanks to modern contraception, are far less likely than in the past to produce children. The biological disadvantages of incest are, of course, nonexistent if the incestuous coupling does not result in offspring, so that we live in a society where there are no practical reasons why brother and sister, for example, should not live together as man and wife, permitted by society to do so as long as they don't actually reproduce. With suitable advances in genetic diagnosis and counselling, there is no real reason why even this final barrier should not be allowed to crumble, permitting some incestuous couples to have normal children. We have so modified our environment that we can even permit this sacrifice of genetic variability, and if conditions change again we can be assured that although those populations that have, for many generations, preferred incest to outbreeding will be unlikely to weather the change there will be plenty of other people around to carry on the human line.

It is just as well that we can see no biological objection to incest in modern society, for those same advances in our abilities that make genetic counselling possible also 'threaten' a growing number of children in our society with unwitting incest. It is becoming routine for doctors to solve the problem of male infertility in an otherwise happy marriage by providing the wife with sperm from an anonymous donor. (Here, indeed, is another solution for the incestuous couple who wish to raise children.) Often such a donor will be an intelligent college male, usually a medical student eager to supplement his income, and he may provide sperm for several inseminations. Although most doctors take care to use several donors, and to avoid concentrating one donor's contributions in one geographical location, there is still a chance that offspring from one donor—half siblings—may meet and marry. Some countries—France, for example—recognise this possibility and insist that sperm from one donor be used only a limited number of times. In other places, notably certain of the United States, the law makes no such provisions. Paradoxically, the risk is greater in states where the technique is less widely practised, because then fewer centres provide this kind of treatment, and they rely on fewer donors. Will this ultimately pose a major problem for society? Probably not, but it requires only the application of some simple rules to make absolutely certain that the problem is minimised.

It is, however, far from clear just what the biological limits to incest might be. Half-sibs, resulting from a widespread artificial insemination programme, might not have a significantly greater chance of producing defective offspring, or then again they might have. Nobody knows, and this biological uncertainty is reflected in the wide variety of cultural taboos on incest. Our own society applies strict constraints only to members of the immediate nuclear family, and in Sweden there are already moves afoot to remove all restrictions. In other cultures a person may be forbidden thousands of otherwise eligible partners who are culturally, although not genetically, relatives. The whole of the mother's clan, for example, might be out of bounds. The most perplexing examples are provided by attitudes to cousins. In some cultures marriages between first cousins are not permitted, while in others such marriages are at least highly desirable and in some cases compulsory.

While cultures may vary as to who exactly is taboo, they all proscribe someone. The avoidance of incest is one of the characteristics of the human species, a characteristic it shares with many other species. The differences between people and other apes on this point do not mean that we avoid incest for cultural reasons and apes for biological reasons, but that human society has created a complex overlay masking the simple biological bases of behaviour.

The kibbutz is abnormal—that is why it is interesting—but it reveals the truth about this facet of human nature. Another example thrusts home the point. In Taiwan a couple may wed as children and be reared together in a practice called Shim-pua marriage. Couples who go through this form of marriage have far more difficulty consummating their liaison, have more extramarital affairs, fewer children, and more divorces than couples who meet and marry at a biologically appropriate age. Mistakes, like this inappropriate application of the incest avoidance mechanism, tell us how a system ought to work if all went well. In this sense, the mistake of homosexuality ought surely to provide us with comparably deep insights into the nature of human behaviour.

Before any irate homosexuals accuse us of imposing our value judgement on their sexual preferences, let us stress again that when we say it is a mistake we mean that any individual that went in exclusively for homosexuality would leave no genes and so would not be an evolutionary success. No individual is an evolutionary success unless it leaves copies of its genes. We do not imply that homosexuality is bad in any absolute moral sense, only that when carried to extremes, and in evolutionary terms, it is a mistake. It might seem that even when not carried to extremes it is a mistake, in this sense, since surely every homosexual act could be replaced by a heterosexual one that offers a chance to reproduce. But the situation must be more complex than this, since homosexuality seems to have been a pervasive, if minority, aspect of human activity throughout history. Something that is exclusively bad, evolutionarily speaking, would not have survived for so many generations, and homosexuality is not even restricted to the human species.

Homosexual behaviour is found occasionally among ducks and geese and in many other animals. Hamadryas baboon troops in the high Semian mountains of Ethiopia contain bands of homosexual bachelors, some of whom behave like females and help the masculine males to ejaculate by masturbating them. The primatologist who watched these particular baboons thinks that there may be a

distinct advantage to all this for the masculine homosexual baboons, because frequent ejaculations keep their levels of testosterone, the male sex hormone, high and so allow them to behave
like normal heterosexual males if they get the opportunity to interact with normal heterosexual females. But he cannot see what is in it
for the masturbator males; perhaps they are simply bullied into
submission.[109]

But despite the occasional homosexual in other primates, homosexuality is more common in man than in other species. Culture too
is a feature of man, so do we need a biological account of homosexuality? It is obviously wrong to assume that homosexuals do not
breed at all; many only discover their preference after the
breakdown of a reproductively successful marriage, while others
are not exclusively homosexual by preference. In fact nobody
knows whether homosexuals are, in the Darwinian sense, less fit
than heterosexuals. Nor do we know for certain whether there is
any genetic basis to homosexuality. Some evidence, gathered from
pairs of twins fostered in separate homes, suggests that there may be
a hereditary basis to homosexuality, but there is certainly no proof
of a 'homosexual gene'. The suggestive evidence on the one hand,
and the possibility of reproductive failure on the other, have led
theorists to develop all sorts of ideas about how homosexuality
might have evolved in our past. Some of the orthodox theories are
quite appealling, but in the absence of any clear need for such a
theory we don't think there is very much point in devoting a lot of
effort to conjuring up 'explanations' of homosexuality. Some
homosexuals, less aware perhaps of the lack of biological evidence
one way or the other, have themselves come up with their own
theory which, regrettably, totally misunderstands the very nature
of evolution.

They say that sexual deviancy is the 'mainspring' that provides
the 'driving force' of evolution, that animals have stopped evolving
and therefore have no need for homosexuality, but that man has
more evolution ahead of him and so has homosexuals who, far from
being aberrant in any way, are vital for our continued evolution.
This is arrant nonsense, for many reasons. Evolution never stops,
by virtue of the simple fact that the potential for reproduction
inevitably outstrips the capacity of the land; there will always be a
struggle to survive, and a few will always be selected from the

many. Evolution needs no mainspring, no driving force, because as long as there is variation and a struggle to survive there will be selection from among the variants and so evolution. Man is not 'higher' or 'more evolved' than any other species, just different. The misguided efforts of homosexuals to justify their existence on biological, and therefore, as they see it, incontrovertibly fundamental, grounds are best ignored. But other aspects of the behaviour of homosexuals are of interest to us.

Two facts about homosexuals are undeniably clear, even in the more enlightened homosexual communities where they are less likely to be the product of harassment by heterosexuals. One is that male homosexuals are astonishingly promiscuous, enjoying casual sex to a far greater degree than most heterosexuals. A survey of homosexuals in San Francisco showed that, among white males, 28 per cent reported having had more than a thousand partners, and 75 per cent said that they had had more than a hundred partners. Not one white female reported having had a thousand partners, and only 2 per cent had had more than a hundred.[110] Similar figures emerge from other surveys. Now, if we accept that there really are differences between men and women in their strategic approach to sex and reproduction, fundamental differences borne of 1,000 million years of evolution since some bacteria first discovered sex, and if we further accept that homosexuals differ from heterosexuals only in their choice of sex object and not in their basic psychological make-up, then what we see in homosexual behaviour might be the expression of pure male or pure female strategies. Heterosexuals must compromise their desires on both sides if partners are to stay together and raise children. But homosexuals have no need to compromise and so should be able to behave without this encumbrance. Their behaviour should therefore show us the undiluted male and female sexual strategies.

What did we find? That female homosexuals are generally monogamous and faithful while male homosexuals are promiscuous. This is precisely what we might expect, because females invest heavily in their offspring and can increase their fitness only by investing even more. Hence monogamy and faithfulness, even in the absence of offspring. Males, with their cheap throwaway sperm, we would expect to be promiscuous; mating costs them little so they should seek sexual opportunities wherever they can. Mixed couples compromise, but homosexuals do seem to show the pure strategy. Donald Symons, the anthropologist who drew attention to this observation, sums his views up like this:

'I am suggesting that heterosexual men would be as likely as homosexual men to have sex most often with strangers, to participate in anonymous orgies in public baths, and to stop off in public restrooms for five minutes of fellatio on the way home from work if women were interested in these activities. But women are not interested.'[111]

This in itself offers one explanation of homosexual behaviour. If women are not interested in casual sexual encounters, the next best thing for a man in search of sexual gratification might be a quickie with another man. On the other side of the sexual divide, women who see men as heartless philanderers can find consolation with one another. Symons puts it slightly differently: 'Among men, sex sometimes results in intimacy; among women, intimacy sometimes results in sex.'[112]

We chose to look in some detail at homosexuality and incest because they each reveal the importance of biology in behaviour. Incest avoidance is not simply a matter of cultural rules and taboos. If it were the children of the kibbutz would have no problems. That they do is testimony to the power of biology over culture. And homosexuality confirms that the differences between male and female sexual strategies are deep-rooted, not the product of cultural influences by 'society' or 'the media'. Homosexual men, according to Martin Daly and Margo Wilson, embrace the larger society's idealisation of monogamy but usually fail in their efforts to achieve it. Something—their maleness—subverts them. They say they do not see anything manly or admirable in fleeting sexual encounters in public places, but they pursue them nevertheless. Don Symons, who opened our eyes to this view of sexuality, must have the last word: 'That homosexual men are at least as likely as heterosexual men to be interested in pornography, cosmetic qualities, and youth seems to me to imply that these interests are no more the result of advertising than adultery and alcohol consumption are the results of country and western music.'[113] In his roundabout, but entertaining, way, Symons is saying that the behaviour typical of males and females, even in our supposedly advanced society, is that way because it is biologically sensible for it to be.

Sex has been an important part of evolutionary history; it is still with us today, and many aspects of present day cultural behaviour are best interpreted by looking at them in an evolutionary light. But that does not mean that our behaviour is set in our genes. There is no imperative that men be unfaithful, or that women be true, and while those tendencies may exist as a result of our evolutionary past, we are free to choose; a knowledge of that past may make it easier for us to choose.

Any guide to behaviour that is based on a consideration of evolution must beware of two things: the evolutionary facts should be correct, and the genetic basis of today's behaviour should be confirmed. If you imagine that early man survived only by being horribly aggressive, and if you imagine that this aggressiveness is still lurking in our DNA, and will express itself no matter what, then you will have a pessimistic view of the future and will excuse any violence today, blaming it on the genes. We don't accept that view at all, both because man's history was in all probability not aggressively violent and because there is no evidence for a genetic basis to aggression. But if you agree with us that sexual reproduction is such a fundamental part of life that its influence is going to be felt in all sorts of ways, but that nevertheless that influence is not absolute, you will realise that although evolution provides an explanation of present-day behaviour, in no way does it justify that behaviour. Biology is not ethics, no matter how much some people would like it to be.

The examples we have discussed in this chapter show how patterns of sexual behaviour that were evolutionarily advantageous remain, not all that well hidden, behind the veil of culture that seems to differentiate peoples from one another, and humans from animals. We have also shown how those same patterns can become scrambled and confused in modern culture. Cultural evolution has leaped ahead of biological evolution, and we are still living through the resulting period of adjustment. But culture isn't everything. We keep saying that man is an animal, even if a cultural animal. The time has come to look at man and woman as animals, and in particular at their physiology as reproductive animals.

OF SEX AND APES

People are uniquely cultural animals, preserving in their oral traditions and social behaviour ways of doing things that go far beyond the biology of their inherited genetic instructions. That those traditions nevertheless make a great deal of sense when seen in an evolutionary perspective is testimony to the fact that the biology of mankind is what makes us cultural. If biology and evolution make such sense of culture, what can they tell us about the machinery of reproduction? We have evolved over millions of years to be the way we are, and an examination of what we are, and how we compare with some of our closest relatives, can tell us much about ourselves. Nowhere is this clearer than in the field of sex and reproduction.

Take the simple matter of size. We have seen that male gametes are small and mobile as an adaptation to exploiting the large stationary eggs produced by females, but what about the animals that produce those gametes? You might be tempted, from everyday experience, to say that the female is generally the smaller sex. She certainly is in many of the mammals with which we are familiar, including, of course, ourselves. But as a generality, this is dead wrong. In insects alone, which outnumber all other animals by many times, the female is almost always the larger; she needs to be to gather the resources that she will put into her eggs. So in the animal kingdom as a whole, females are larger than males. And if you think insects are irrelevant to ourselves, at least in this particular debate, consider this: there are many mammals in which the female is larger, and some taxonomic groups in which larger females are the rule. Rabbits and hares, bats, seals and antelopes all have larger females. So do baleen whales, and that makes a very interesting point. Katherine Ralls, from the Smithsonian Institution in Washington DC, points out that because the blue whale is the largest animal that ever lived, and because female blue whales are larger than males, the largest animal ever to have lived was a female.[114]

But among people, men are bigger than women.[115] The

average difference in height is about 8 per cent, slightly less than in chimpanzees, but there is considerable variation. Least different are the pygmies of Central Africa, in whom males are just 4.7 per cent bigger than females. Most different are the Tarahumara, a tribe of American Indians who live in southwestern Chihuahua in northern Mexico. The men of the Tarahumara are 11.6 per cent taller than the women. But despite the variation, in all groups of people the average man is taller than the average woman, the exact opposite of the situation in most of the animal kingdom. Why? The one factor that tends, more than any other, to select for larger males, and hence for the possibility of males eventually becoming larger than females, is competition, competition between males over mates, in which large size can be a distinct advantage. And competition implies a degree of polygyny, because males who are more success-ful in the struggle will gain more mates than losers. The red deer provides a classic example. So what does the simple size difference between men and women tell us about the mating system in which early man evolved?

We have already seen, from an examination of marriage patterns and mating behaviour, that mankind today is mildly polygynous, with many men having just a single wife but some managing two or three. The so-called sexual dimorphism in size supports this con-clusion. If we look at a group of animals in detail, we find a distinct correlation between the degree of sexual dimorphism and the average harem size. In seals and hoofstock, for example, species with proportionately bigger males also have bigger harems. And in primates too, bigger males are associated with more polygyny. Calculating the association from 22 species, and then looking to find where *Homo sapiens* 'ought' to be, we discover that, with his average excess height of about 8 per cent, man should have an average harem size of between two and three, very close to the true state of affairs.[116]

The variation in human sexual dimorphism could also be reveal-ing, because it might be possible to pick up a link between the degree of polygyny and the size difference *within* a single species, rather than by comparing a number of species, and we could con-sider this even more convincing. In general, American Indians are the most dimorphic humans and Africans and New Guineans the least, with Europeans and Asians in the middle. Unfortunately

Africans and New Guineans, despite having the smallest size difference between men and women, also seem to have the greatest difference between successful and unsuccessful men, the exact reverse of our expectation. But there are many other factors that influence size difference besides mating system, and perhaps even more that affect the mating system itself. To get an insight into these Richard Alexander and his colleagues at the University of Michigan in Ann Arbor divided monogamous cultures into two groups. On the one hand were those societies in which monogamy was a cultural rule, with some pressure in its favour but probably quite a lot of evasion on the quiet. On the other hand were the societies on whom ecological considerations imposed monogamy. These are generally people who live in places that are poor in essentials, in which they would find it very difficult to gather the resources needed to breed. This latter type of monogamy, Alexander argues, might be more typical of the monogamy found in nature, and his comparisons show that 'ecologically imposed' monogamy is linked with a much lower level of size difference than both 'socially imposed' monogamy and polygamy.[117] Where nature favours monogamy, and males do not compete, the sexes are more alike.

Size difference, then, places mankind in the mildly polygynous compartment of the animal kingdom. It thus agrees with so many other observations that suggest that men, rather than women, have the capacity to do either much better, or much worse, than average in the reproductive race. The tallness of men joins the fact that they take longer to mature, that they suffer higher mortality, that they age more quickly, and that they receive more parental care as yet another indicator that mild polygyny was the customary state of affairs in our evolutionary past. (We need hardly add that this does not, of itself, excuse the behaviour of men who flaunt society's rules; biology is not an excuse for bad behaviour.)

Rules, like males being bigger when mating is polygynous, help us to make sense of the variety of life. Of course there is variety too in the credence people put in rules and whether they apply to the human species. Tim Halliday, an expert on amphibian sex, does not think that the size difference between men and women reflects polygyny in our past. 'The sturdier physique of men,' he writes, 'is likely to have been much more important in enabling him to fulfil his parental role in a mating alliance than in disputes between men for the possession of women.'[118] So not everyone accepts the rules.

Exceptions, too, are useful for testing rules, and not surprisingly there are exceptions to this particular rule. As we said, mating system is seldom the only influence on male size; competition with other males might favour bigger males, but other factors may select against large size. Monkeys provide a good example. Sexual dimorphism is indeed related to degree of polygyny, but not as strongly as in some other groups. When you look closely at the data, you find that monkeys that live on the ground have disproportionately more dimorphism than monkeys that live in trees. Male ground-dwelling monkeys, such as baboons, are bigger than they should be.[119] (Or perhaps male tree dwellers, such as black and white colobus monkeys, are smaller than they should be; it is all relative.) The reason is obvious, once you think about it. On the ground, being bigger is, quite simply, better. In the trees, being bigger is better up to a point, but beyond that point you get so heavy you start to break branches, and bones. So ecological considerations keep arboreal males small.

Food is another factor that can distort sexual dimorphism. There aren't any good examples from the primates, but among birds, male and female members of the same monogamous species may be quite different in order to exploit different foods. On the islands of the Caribbean there are woodpeckers where males and females have very different beaks.[120] These differences allow the birds to feed in very different styles—one sex probing for hidden insects, the other gleaning for exposed food—which means that the two members of a monogamous pair do not compete with one another for food on their joint territory.

But perhaps the most important exception to the rule of big being better in males, at least from our biased vertebrate viewpoint, is when the competition between males is not settled by a physical struggle. Male weddell seals, although highly polygynous, are smaller than females. Weddell seals are also peculiar in that they mate in the water, not on land. So a male's success at mating many females will depend more on his agility than on brute force.[121] Turtles are the same.[122] In those species that mate on land, males fight and are bigger than females. Mating in the water, agility and elaborate display count for more and males are smaller than females. But let us return to our own species. The exact nature of the competition between males explains a delightful anatomical difference between man and his nearest relatives, the chimpanzee and gorilla.

The gorilla troop is the domain of a dominant male who, because of the grey hair that covers his back and flanks, is known as a silverback.[123] The silverback, with his enormous crested skull, is physically much more imposing than his females; he is 30 per cent taller and almost twice as heavy as his females. A successful silverback attracts young females to join his harem, and patrols a home range in which other male gorillas are not welcome. Certainly no adult male other than the dominant silverback ever gets close enough to the females of the troop to sire offspring. So gorilla fathers suffer no great uncertainty about the paternity of their children, and are evolutionarily happy to invest in their well-being. Adolescent males drift away from the troop to set up their own territory, and try to attract young females from other groups, but most males never gain a harem. The adult females show little inclination to leave their protector, and eventually a young adult male, often a son of the ageing silverback, takes over as leader of the troop.

We don't know what it is that attracts a female to a particular male. Perhaps his territory contains a lot of good food, or perhaps it is something about the male himself—his silver back, for example. But we do know that gorilla society is extremely well ordered and peaceful, females and their children enjoying the protection of a strong and powerful male, made so by competition with other males in his evolutionary past. The silverback, in exchange for his protection, enjoys exclusive access to those females for breeding. We also know that, for their size, silverback gorillas have the smallest testes of any primate.[124] The relevance of this seemingly bizarre comment will be apparent when we have discussed chimpanzee society.

Considering that they share more than 99 per cent of their DNA, a bigger contrast in lifestyle than that between chimps and gorillas can hardly be imagined.[125] Males contribute very little to family life. The adults live in a largish troop of about ten individuals, but go around in smaller shifting coalitions. The troop as a whole defends a large territory against neighbouring troops of chimpanzees and within this homeland are several females and their families. Each female, with her immature offspring, also keeps a territory within the group homeland but it is small and partially overlaps the neighbouring females' space. When a female chimp comes on heat she develops a visual signal, a swollen bottom, and emits powerful scents, pheromones, that attract males from miles around. One male may, if he is persistent and lucky, and if she co-operates by keeping quiet, succeed in taking the female off for a few days on what primatologists call a consortship. He will try to keep her away from other males and will mount her as often as he can during this time. Being a consort must be quite a successful strategy because studies in the wild reveal that about half of all chimpanzees are conceived when their mothers have a consort.[126] The other males seem to know this too, and will often attack a consort when he rejoins the group.[127] In any event, while consortships account for half of all newborn chimpanzees, the remainder are conceived as a result of male behaviour that can best be described as a gang bang.

Any male worth the name will cluster round a receptive female and attempt to mount her. There is a pecking order among the males which decides, for example, who gets the best food, but this has very little influence on who mounts the female and indeed she doesn't seem to express any strong preference either. For a period of a few days, while the female is on heat, there is total chaos, during which the female will have been mounted several times by each male in the troop. Neither she nor the males have any idea who fathered her offspring, so it is hardly surprising that the males contribute nothing to the upbringing of the child. Individually, no male knows which infants he has sired and no male pays any infant particular attention. Collectively, they defend all the females and their infants from the attentions of other males. The males of a chimpanzee troop do not fight much among themselves, nor do they protect the females and young directly, so they are not much bigger or stronger than females. But they do compete in more subtle ways. The way to gain an advantage in a gang bang is to produce more sperm than the next male, because then your sperm is more likely to fertilise the waiting egg, and this is exactly what chimpanzees do. Their testicles are enormous, much bigger than those of either man or gorilla.

Relative to its body weight the chimpanzee has the biggest testicles of any primate; they weigh 120 grams, and constitute 0.3 per cent of its body weight. Gorillas, whose sperm do not have to compete at all, have minute testicles in proportion, still 35 grams but ten times smaller, relative to their body weight, than a chimpanzee's. Man's testes are somewhere between those two extremes, weighing in at between 25 and 50 grams, 0.04 to 0.08 per cent of his body weight. The number of sperms in each ejaculation tells the same story: chimpanzees release 600 million, men 250 million, and gorillas just 50 million.[128]

The size of the male's penis is another anatomical quirk. Gorillas have very small penes indeed. Having dominion over their females they have no need for any kind of sexual display, and the penis is more than adequate for its basic task of putting the semen where it is needed. Chimps, by contrast, have a relatively large penis which is decorated on its underside with a broad white stripe. This stripe continues down the penis and on to the scrotum, and has the effect of accentuating the length of the erect penis. Male chimpanzees use the erect penis as a sexual and aggressive display, and a long penis may also be of some assistance in the gang bang sexual scramble by placing the sperm as close to the egg as possible. But man has by far the largest penis of any primate. It is unlikely that the purpose of man's large penis is primarily as a signal, though it may have been put to that use in some cultures now and in the past, because the erect penis is generally regarded as a very private thing. Some biologists think that the penis has lengthed to cope with face to face copulation, which in turn promotes long-term bonding between male and female who can gaze on one another's faces. This, as we shall see, ignores the fact that other primates that form pairs do not have either large penes or face to face copulation. Perhaps the large penis exists to stimulate the female. In one sense this is very doubtful, because the depths of the vagina are almost as insensitive as the shaft of the penis. It is for this reason that penis size is completely irrelevant to the degree of sexual stimulation experienced by a woman, at least statistically. Obviously some women do find bigger better, but equally others are hurt by a large penis. Overall, though, there is no evidence of a relationship between penis size and pleasure.[129] But although the differences in penis size among men might be irrelevant, the large size of man's penis compared to that of the other apes could be related to stimulation of the female, because sex has assumed a much more pleasurable existence in man than in the other apes. Again, however, this sounds like special pleading; sex may be pleasurable now, but was it during the evolution of man's large penis? We don't know, and may never be able satisfactorily to explain this particular human peculiarity.

Female apes too have their differences, and these mirror the differences we have seen among the males. A chimpanzee broadcasts far and wide her sexual availability; she wants as many males as possible to compete for the privilege of siring her children because in that way she ensures that her children will get half of their genes from a vigorous and successful male. (Also, if each male might be the father they will all have an interest in defending the troop as a whole.) A gorilla female, by contrast, hardly advertises her sexual state at all. She has an assuredly successful father for her children, and although the silverback seems to know when a female is receptive there are few signs easily visible from afar. Researchers who watch gorillas have to keep a careful eye on the male's behaviour to discover when the females are in heat.

The chimpanzee exemplifies the original sexual strategy, the male pouring his resources into vast numbers of gametes and the female accepting those gametes without choice. Gorillas show an altered pattern. The silverback achieves the same end as the chimpanzee by putting his resources into territorial defence and monopolising his females, who benefit from this male investment in a steady and protected home range. Where do humans fall? Our extra size indicates that for millions of years at least part of our reproductive effort went into direct competition against other males. How much our sperm compete is very hard to say because no one has really studied us in the same way as the apes have been studied. But one of the major differences between us and the African apes is that human females do not come into heat. The human species seems to have neatly separated sexual receptivity from reproductive fertility. A woman will accept a man's sexual advances at any time in her menstrual cycle, unlike the apes, and although the period of maximum fertility remains the day or so just after the egg has been released, normally halfway through the cycle, babies can be conceived on any day of the cycle. This difference needs to be explained. Why have people evolved this way?

The first thing to note is that the very name given to this phenomenon reflects the attitude of those doing the explaining. For many years now this aspect of human female behaviour has been called continual receptivity, a name that begins by establishing a male viewpoint and begging for an answer in those terms. More recently it is coming to be known as sequestered (or hidden) ovulation, which sees things more from the female's side, though not exclusively so, and demands a different sort of explanation.

Originally, the human female's continual receptivity was seen as a device that she used to strengthen the pair bond.[130] Copulation was a reward to the male to keep him with her and help her to raise the offspring. The argument was that the woman's loss of a defined period of oestrus meant that she would automatically give her male an increased number of copulations, and this was selected by evolution because it kept man and woman together. Although this is a plausible enough story, which held sway for many years, and still holds sway in some quarters, it is almost certainly yet another case of special pleading by men. The reason is so simple that we wonder why the idea of sex as an inducement to keep the male at home ever gained the credence it did. Quite simply, what has sex to do with staying together? Having a male around to share parental duties can be very advantageous in the right circumstances, and that is why we do see monogamous species. But the male will be selected to do this because of the fitness he gains, the extra this behaviour contributes to the survival of his own genes. No further reward is needed. Or, if it is, it should be needed by males of all species, not just human males. As Devra Kleiman, an ethologist at the National Zoo in Washington, DC, has pointed out, other mammals that have long-term pair bonds between a couple are, if anything, less sexually active and have a more defined oestrus than species that don't form pair bonds.[131] The gorilla is sexually much less active than the chimpanzee, and even though monogamous pair bonds are not involved, a long-term relationship is. And the lesser apes, gibbons and siamangs, which are monogamous for life, are sexually very inactive; siamangs copulate during just four months every two and a half years. Richard Alexander and Katherine Noonan, in their survey of the problem, put this objection very well: 'Constant sex,' they write, 'is a useless and potentially dangerous distraction from the business of staying live and healthy and raising one's offspring.'[132] So we need some other reason for the divorce of receptivity from fertility, one that does not make an exception of man; the one that we favour is further evidence of the Machiavellian politics of sex, but we can learn something from the accounts that we dismiss.

A more modern version of the reward theory says that females are perpetually receptive because only by being so can they conceal their true ovulatory state. If receptivity and fertility were more or less simultaneous, as they are in almost every other species, the male could effectively protect his investment in the female by sequestering her only when she was on heat. The rest of the time she could wander freely and he would not risk being cuckolded. This could be to the males' benefit if females were easily able to rear infants on their own, but in fact the human infant needs a great deal of care and the extra investment provided by males, and society, makes all the difference to infant survival. A female who is receptive even when she is not fertile ensures that she will enjoy the protection and assistance of a monopolising male partner.

This is essentially the thinking used by Owen Lovejoy, an anatomist at Kent State University in Ohio, to spin a fanciful hypothesis of the origins of upright walking. It takes as its starting point a monogamous relationship between male and female and what he says is the very slow rate of reproduction of the great apes.[133] In Lovejoy's view, the extended receptivity of the female does indeed hide her fertility, but she does so to prevent other males from finding her attractive. Her own mate, of course, finds her attractive, but this is the result of individualised signals rather than the pheromones that signal a free-for-all. 'The development of stimulating systems that are specific to individuals is called epigamic differentiation,' Lovejoy says. 'I call it being in love.'[134] And because he finds her attractive, the human male walks upright and with his hands free brings food back to his loved female back at their base camp. With this extra provisioning for their child, and freed from unwanted harassment by other males, she can reproduce more often, and so people, rather than the other apes, spread to cover the world.

This is all very well, but it doesn't actually explain what it sets out to. We can see that the female can avoid the interfering attentions of other males if she does conceal her fertility, but why should she do this by being continually receptive? Why not be like other long-bonded species and have a private signal between the members of the pair? The best Lovejoy can manage takes us back where we started. The female is continually receptive, he says, because it keeps the male interested in her, keeps bringing him back, with gifts of food for the female to help provision their offspring. It should be obvious that there is a major problem with this notion; it is wide open to cheats. Any rogue male that, signals or no, attempts to inseminate any females he comes across will be a roaring success. (Some men today are habitual rapists; we regard this as a pathology, as evolution gone wrong perhaps, and will not deal with the problem further.) Some other male will provide the food that helps his infant succeed. Pretty soon all the males will be philanderers, and the problem Lovejoy set out to solve, that of providing enough food for females, by providing faithful, bipedal, provisioning males, will be back in full force.

Another major flaw in the argument is that Lovejoy supposes that ovulation is as hidden from the female as it is from himself, the male. If he didn't, there would be no need for him to explain continual receptivity by saying 'she'd better keep him interested, because she's fertile for only about three days. If she copulates once every two weeks her chance of getting pregnant is pretty low. She can't afford that. It's her job to get pregnant quickly, as soon as she can handle the next infant.'[135] The truth is that women can often be quite well aware of when they ovulate. Most western women are not, it is true, but this is because they do not pay attention to their bodies. But thanks to the feminist movement, which has reawakened women's self-awareness and taught them how to interpret their own bodies, this is increasingly no longer the case. Some women experience a distinct sensation around the time of ovulation. This is called *Mittelschmerz* because it is a pain in the middle of the cycle.[136] But even for women who do not feel *Mittelschmerz* there are clear signs associated with ovulation; a woman's temperature rises and her vaginal mucus becomes clear, slippery, and watery. Once she has learned to detect these signs a woman can be as aware of her time of maximum fertility as any animal in oestrus. And even if she is not consciously aware of ovulation, a woman's behaviour changes in all sorts of ways, some sexual and some not. As one example, a careful watch on the women arriving at an American discotheque, coupled with some discreet questioning afterwards, revealed that the ones who were in the middle of their menstrual cycle wore more make-up and jewellery and were touched by men more often than women at other stages of the cycle.[137]

These are just some of the objections to this newest account of why the human female does not display a discrete period of oestrus. Others surfaced in a collection of published comments[138] from other workers in many different fields, who challenged Lovejoy from the standpoints of their own specialities on everything from his data and assumptions to his jocular use of a 'personal communication' from his friend Don Johanson, the famous fossil hunter, as evidence that 'human females are continually sexually receptive'.[139] The end result seems to be that Lovejoy's theory, and others like it, are not being taken very seriously.

So if Lovejoy's male-oriented version of continual receptivity (even if he does occasionally call it sequestered ovulation) is no good, what is the correct account? Could it be, as Donald Symons and Randy Thornhill have both suggested, that concealed ovulation is valuable to a woman because it allows her to cuckold her mate? By hiding her ovulation from the male, the female diminishes her mate's ability to hide her only when she is most valuable to him. He has to protect her, and her infants, all the time, but to do this at all successfully and monopolise the female would occupy an inordinate amount of the male's resources and time, far too much to make it worthwhile for most men. Many a female, they suggest, will find herself in a long-term alliance with a male not to her liking; having a concealed ovulation gives her the opportunity to be fertilised by the male of her own choice, the freedom to mate with a male not her husband. There could be an advantage, at the genetic level, in a female having her children fathered by more than one male. (As we shall see, variety itself may be a good thing.) It doesn't matter if the father of some of her offspring is a philanderer—provided the children are raised by a mug. This is because her sons, being hereditary philanderers themselves, will then spread their genes, and hers, far and wide. But then, where will the next generation of mugs come from?

The answer is that in the real world human males are neither completely faithful nor unadulterated philanderers. Evolution has selected men who are faithful providers for their families most of the time but are not averse to taking advantage of the opportunity to father children by other women. Most men are both philanderer and mug, depending on circumstances, and this ambivalent behaviour is characteristic of the way nature operates. Whenever evolution is presented with this kind of simple choice—whether to be brave or cowardly, faithful or philanderer, hunter or parasite—the solution will be a mixture of the two strategies. Neither one on its own is stable, for a mutant who pursues the opposite strategy, a hawk in a world of doves or a mug in a world of philanderers, will do relatively better than the others. The mug will do better because the extra parental care he contributes will enable him to raise more offspring than the majority, composed of philanderers who abandon their mates. When all men are mugs a philanderer does better because he puts his effort into getting women pregnant, not into caring for the results. The evolutionary solution may be to have a proportion of the population being philanderers and the remainder mugs, or to be a philanderer on some occasions and a mug on others, but the answer will almost always be a mixture of strategies. And by making certain assumptions about the costs and benefits associated with each strategy it is possible to calculate the eventual balance between the strategies.

Richard Dawkins at Oxford University's Animal Behaviour Research Group has worked out the possibilities for the case of mugs *versus* philanderers.[140] Using one particular set of assumptions, he finds that a breeding group will eventually settle down into a stable mixture of fast and faithful types—8 fast to 5 faithful as it happens—at which ratio the two types do equally well. The calculations cannot say whether there will be 5 mugs to every 8 philanderers, or whether each male will be a mug on 5 occasions and a philanderer on 8, as the two options are exactly equivalent, but the point is well enough made; in this sort of set-up there is inevitably a balance between cheats and honest citizens, so there will always be a supply of philanderers, and a supply of mugs to make it worthwhile philandering. While it might be possible for females, by separating receptivity from fertility, to separate the nurturant duties of a father from his genetic duties, this is probably rather unreliable and in any case is liable to be rather unstable. We don't think that female sexuality evolved because it allows a woman to dupe her male.

Another suggestion is that by keeping quiet about her fertility a female avoids the brouhaha that attends oestrus in other species. This again begs the question. Why should it be a good thing for female chimps to attract males from far and wide, while female humans benefit by keeping quiet? We must go beyond the simple statement and show why a quiet ovulation is a good thing. A final idea, interesting but probably unimportant, is that the target of the female's deception is not the male but herself. Nancy Burley, of the University of Illinois, thinks that pregnancy, childbirth and motherhood are so traumatic, so unrewarding, that a woman would avoid getting pregnant if she possibly could.[141] Females who did avoid getting pregnant would leave fewer descendants than those who got pregnant. This, clearly, would be a bad thing, but it might happen if women's emerging consciousness and self awareness made them leery of the consequences of copulation. For an animal to succeed it must reproduce, and one way that this might be achieved against the wishes of an unwilling consciousness is for evolution to render the woman unaware of her reproductive status. She then has a choice between celibacy and running the risk of pregnancy, and Burley believes that she is not capable of celibacy. Sex, and reproduction, ensue. Woman, Burley suggests, has been selected to fool herself, thereby getting sex and the occasional pregnancy.

Having dealt with some of the ideas that have been advanced to account for this unique aspect of the human female, and their shortcomings, we should perhaps be prepared to tell our own story about the evolution of concealed ovulation and continual receptivity. Perhaps the most important thing to stress is that the phenomenon is by no means as absolute as it sounds. We have already mentioned the ways in which a woman might be aware of her own fertility. To these can be added observations that female sexuality is by no means constant over the menstrual cycle. Women initiate sexual activities with men almost twice as often on the day of ovulation as on other days. And they masturbate nearly three times more often at mid-cycle than at other times. So while there may not be an all-or-none period of intense sexual activity, as characterises other animals, there is a definite peaking around the time of maximum fertility.[142] Oestrus is not lost, though it is partially hidden. The second point concerns receptivity. A female chimp is indeed receptive when in oestrus; she will accept any and every male who approaches. A female person may be able, and willing, to accept her mate at any time, but that does not mean she is continually receptive to all men. Quite the reverse. Frank Beach, doyen of sex researchers, put it very well: 'No human female is "constantly sexually receptive". (Any male who entertains this illusion must be a very old man with a short memory or a very young man due for a bitter disappointment.)'[143]

So we are left with more or less hidden ovulation and a continual receptivity to the right male. How could these be valuable to an evolving early human? We need a situation in which some males are providing some parental care. When that is so, prominent ovulation would be a handicap for two reasons. First, it would attract rival males. These would be around because early human society almost certainly consisted of bands of several males and their mates and offspring. The males would co-operate to hunt and to defend the band, and competition between them for matings would disrupt this co-operation. So it would be in the female's interest to avoid fostering competition, provided that she is getting some parental help from one particular male, her mate. One way to do this is to avoid broadcasting her fertility. Another way is to ensure that all the females in the band come into oestrus at the same time. That way there are too many available females for any male to monopolise, and hence little competition. This is what lions do. It may also be what people do, though to a more limited extent. Women who share an office or a dormitory often end up with their menstrual cycles in step.[144] Furthermore, if rival males did copulate with a female, this would severely diminish her partner's confidence in his paternity, which would mitigate against parental care by the male. Secondly, by reducing the period during which he needs to guard her, obvious ovulation in the female would free the male to go off and seek extra-marital matings when his own mate is not fertile. These matings might then result in offspring who would compete for the male's parental attention. Under these circumstances a female who was receptive for a little longer than average, and whose fertility was a little more concealed than average, could induce a male to invest more in guarding her. As he becomes more confident of his paternity, so he would be more willing to look after and provide for the offspring. As a result, he and his mate would do better, and there would be selection for longer, and more selective, receptivity: for more closely concealed ovulation in the female; and for faithfulness in both partners. The change in woman's outward signs of sexual availability could tip man's evolutionary scales away from philandering and in favour of fathering.

Our own version, which brings some of the simpler notions together and draws on Alexander and Noonan[145] quite heavily, is the best we can come up with at the moment. It doesn't, we confess, have that really convincing ring that attracts us to an hypothesis, but it does at least have the merit of being consistent with the rest of the animal world and not pleading a special case for mankind. In truth, we know of no really plausible evolutionary account of either the continual receptivity or sequestered ovulation unique to the human female. Perhaps we will never know of one, but that does not mean that we have to make do with less than adequate ideas, most of which are shot full of holes and rely on special pleading for *Homo sapiens*.

Orgasm provides another tangled knot that we must attempt to undo rather than cut through. The facts of the matter seem simple enough. In men, orgasm comprises the suite of changes that accompany ejaculation of the semen. As such it is essential for fertilisation, and is probably shared in one form or another with males of all other species. In women, things are not so straightforward. We will discuss them in detail below, but for now, it must suffice to say that human females seem at first glance to be the only animals that display anything like the male orgasm, and that is the difference we have to account for. Orgasm is a subject close to many people's hearts, and the source of a great deal of worry, primarily for women but also for those men who care about what their women worry about. The more 'modern' magazines seem to be chock-a-block with articles about the female orgasm: are you getting them, if not why not, how many you need, and so on. Hans Eysenck, the notorious psychologist, reports that 'in parts of California there are lunchtime meetings of women in prestigious hotels to discuss techniques of masturbation as a way of dealing with orgasm difficulties—the modern equivalent of the pottery, yoga and flower-arrangement classes that used to absorb the spare time of suburban housewives'.[146] Female orgasm is a hot topic. Indeed, we think that one reason for the original enormous success of Elaine Morgan's book *The Descent of Woman*, which championed Sir Alister Hardy's view that people evolved their unique attributes by the seaside, was that it homed in on orgasms. Morgan told women that they were being deprived of their orgasms by a combination of men and evolution, the latter having adjusted our anatomy and the former having failed to adjust their own behaviour to that adjustment. She laid most of women's ills at the door of not enough orgasms. There clearly is something to be explained about the female orgasm, and in doing so we will try to be fair, once again taking the whole animal kingdom as our source.

First, another look at the facts of the phenomenon. There is no precise definition, but a great deal of popular agreement, as to what constitutes a female orgasm; something to do with paroxysms and uncontrollable muscular contractions, a bit like a sneeze but apparently of more importance. Hans Eysenck describes it thus: 'Psychologically, it is experienced as an intense, climactic thrill following a build-up of excitement centred in the genital area, and leading to an aftermath of perfect relaxation and contentment. Physiologically, it may be observed as a peak in heart rate of up to about 180 beats per minute (compared with the usual 60 to 80), a similarly doubled or even trebled respiration rate together with irregularity and gasping, and contractions of the anal sphincter. There are also contractions in other muscles, most notably the genitals themselves, but also the neck, arms, legs, back and buttocks. Blood pressure is raised, the skin becomes flushed, the face is contorted into an "agonized" grimace and vocal noises are likely to be emitted, particularly by women.'[147]

Whatever it is, most female mammals do not show any sign of behaviour during copulation that we would recognise as an orgasm. On the other hand, people are not very good at recognising orgasms anyway. The one thorough study of orgasm in non-human primates discovered that female chimps, with a great deal of manual assistance from the experimenter, exhibited all the physiological changes associated with orgasm in female humans. And yet, the two male scientists report, 'a female colleague who observed several experimental sessions found it incredible that this female chimpanzee was experiencing anything even approaching the emotion characteristic of orgasm in women. This may explain much of the subjective evidence against orgasm.'[148] Men, too, are not all that good at discriminating between genuine and faked orgasms.

There is also an enormous variation in the human female's potential for orgasm. Some women, about 10 per cent of the population, never have an orgasm; others have several whenever they have intercourse. (There is no evidence of any difference at all between the husbands of women who do not have orgasms and those who do. It is not, as is so commonly imagined, the man's problem or fault.)[149] Then again, some women consider intercourse without orgasm a waste of time while others pay scant attention to whether or not they have an orgasm. This huge variability is odd. It suggests that female orgasm is perhaps not a product of evolution with a specific function, for if it were it would surely be far less variable than it is. There is no good evidence for one of the myths that does ascribe a function to it; copulation is no more likely to result in conception if the female has an orgasm than if she does not. Indeed, the reverse may be true. It was noticed some time ago that there is a link between the frequency with which women have orgasms and their chances of aborting. In other words, abortion is most prevalent in the same age group in which orgasms are experienced most often, which suggests that the muscular contractions experienced during an orgasm could cause a pregnant woman to go into labour and lose her fetus. William Masters and Virginia Johnson certainly agree. In their exhaustive report on *The Human Sexual Response* they note that women tend to be less concerned with copulation and erotica towards the end of pregnancy. That is not to say that they do not copulate at that time, just that they are less likely to experience an orgasm. So, far from female orgasm being essential for reproduction, it seems to be a distinct hazard, at least during the final three months of pregnancy.

Despite the disconcerting lack of uniformity, it has been suggested that orgasm is nature's reward to the female for enduring the male's advances.[150] This ties in with the idea that continual receptivity is a device to keep men attached to their women; in exchange for faithfulness, and to encourage her actually to receive his advances, natural selection has conferred orgasm on women. Taking a stand similar to Nancy Burley's on concealed ovulation, Eysenck says that 'if women were never to experience the pleasure of an orgasm and the feeling of complete and utter contentment which follows, they might be less motivated to engage in sex.'[151] He goes further, and points out that the occasional elusiveness of the female orgasm puts her on what behaviourists like B. F. Skinner call an intermittent reinforcement schedule. This means that she gets the reward on some of the occasions on which she performs the behaviour, but not on others; rats and pigeons exposed to this kind of timetable end up having a much stronger habit than those given a reward every time they press a bar or peck a key. In other words, women have orgasms, but not every time they copulate, because that makes them even more willing to accept a man's advances.

We don't think this story is very likely, again because it sets man apart from the mainstream of life. Just as they are not continually receptive, so too other monogamous apes show no signs of being more open to orgasm. All this negativity is very frustrating; can we come up with no satisfying evolutionary account of the human female's orgasm?

Perhaps the most interesting thing about the female orgasm is that it is so similar to the male. This is true of the physiology, even down to the vagina and penis contracting at about the same rate, once every 0.8 seconds. It is also—believe it or not—true of the psychological experience. Now it is notoriously difficult to discover what another person is experiencing, but Ellen Vance and Nathaniel Wagner used an ingenious questionnaire technique to investigate the perception of orgasm, and whether it differed between the sexes.[152] Vance and Wagner had students write down descriptions of orgasm, and then went through their replies carefully removing any loaded words such as husband or penis that might betray the gender of the author. They presented a cleaned up list of 48 such descriptions to several psychologists, expert gynaecologists and medical students, asking them simply to indicate whether the description came from a man or a woman. None of the subjects could discriminate between male and female descriptions of orgasm. Rather than meaning that the experts don't know their job, this result suggests that the experience of orgasm is very similar indeed in men and women.

Now that is very interesting. No doubt it is partly because the basic anatomical apparatus is the same in men and women, but the similarity of experience suggests something deeper than mere anatomy. Given the difficulty we all have in describing an orgasm, and telling the real article from a fake in women, why should the two sexes actually be so similar? Perhaps because the woman uses orgasm to signal her sexual satisfaction to her mate. She might be selected to do this if it enhanced the male's confidence in his paternity by reassuring him that his partner did not seek sex elsewhere. One primary difference between men and women is that men must endure a rest before they are capable of a second orgasm, while women are capable of many orgasms in a row. So to the man an orgasm is a sign that copulation has taken place, and will not be able to take place again for a while. The female, signalling as she does that she too has had an orgasm in much the same way as he has, might be indicating that she will not be seeking sexual activity with someone else.

If this is right, and we make no great claim that it is, it will have some interesting consequences. The woman will be able to deceive the man, as indeed she can. More to the point, she will be more likely to have an orgasm with a male who is indeed committed to her and her offspring. There is some evidence that this is the case.[153] Furthermore, she should be more willing to signal satisfaction—real or faked—to a dominant male who is able to offer superior parental benefits. Perhaps this is the basis of the remark widely attributed to Henry Kissinger, that power is the ultimate aphrodisiac.

In the end, however, we confess that, as with concealed ovulation, we don't really understand the evolutionary basis of the human female's capacity for orgasm. Orgasm or something like it seems to be potentially available to most female mammals, and has occasionally been seen not only in captive monkeys but also in some other species. Unlike humans, however, there is little evidence that females of all other species ever show signs of orgasm. Humans differ from other species, partly in their anatomy and partly in their behaviour, in ways that make orgasm much more prevalent in human females than among other species. And that is probably all there is to the mystery; female orgasm is simply a byproduct of our evolution, but one that has been seized upon and elaborated in our various cultures. Rather than our peculiar anatomy *depriving* women of orgasms, as Elaine Morgan argues, it may be that our peculiar anatomy *causes* human females to experience orgasm more often than the females of other species. This interpretation is supported by the observation that no long-established culture that we know of regards female orgasm as an automatic consequence of intercourse. The couple has to work at it, and whether they do so or not is a product of their social, not their evolutionary, history. Some cultures, like the Cook Islanders in the Pacific, allegedly give the young boys instruction in lovemaking, complete with a practical exam conducted by an experienced older woman.[154] Others, like our own, provide almost nothing in the way of training. Orgasm seems to be available to all female mammals, but human females, by virtue of their culture, enjoy it more often than any other species.

We have dealt with some of the more important aspects of human sex, but there remain one or two small puzzles. The female breast is one. Breasts are no more than highly evolved sweat glands, modified for the purpose of manufacturing a nourishing food for the young. All female mammals have them, but in all species other than man the mammary glands are enlarged only when the female has to provide her young with milk. The rest of the time they regress and are quite small. Women's mammary glands do enlarge during and after pregnancy, but they are also quite prominent the rest of the time. Why?

Desmond Morris advanced one of the more famous ideas in his book *The Naked Ape*. Female breasts resemble buttocks, and serve to arouse the male in the new face-to-face position necessitated by the anatomical changes associated with walking upright. By moving a sexual signal from back to front, evolution ensured that early men would not lose interest in copulation. Maybe so. Or maybe not. Elaine Morgan thinks that the breast became enlarged in order to give the infant something to hold on to while it floated in the water waiting for predators to go away. But this does not explain why women's mammary glands are enlarged even when they are not nursing children. Perhaps the answer is that in their evolutionary past they were always nursing. In truth we don't have the faintest idea what evolutionary advantage was bestowed on women with permanently enlarged breasts, although once the change had taken place the breasts were clearly open to use by all sorts of systems in all sorts of ways.

And while we are on the subject of breasts, it is worth making a little detour to consider evolutionary evidence on the question of nursing. Should babies be fed on demand or on a schedule, and if on a schedule, how often? A survey of many mammals shows a clear relationship between the composition of the milk and the frequency with which the mother feeds the young.[155] At one extreme are deer, which feed twice a day and whose rich milk contains 20 per cent fat. At the other are animals like the brown bear, which feed their young more or less continuously. Bear milk is much more dilute, containing just 3 per cent fat. Human milk contains about 4 per cent fat, and so puts our species in the category of demand feeding; that is, the infant regulates when and how much it will feed. A look at foragers like the !Kung San of the Kalahari desert reveals that this is exactly what human mothers do. The !Kung baby has unlimited access to the nipple, and tends to nurse for a minute or two at a time every quarter of an hour or so. One result of this frequent sucking is to prevent the woman becoming fertile again—so-called lactational amenorrhea—which in turn ensures that one child is independent and that the mother has sufficient resources to sustain another pregnancy before she becomes pregnant again. Indeed, although women today regard regular menstruation as a sign that all is well, and in a sense it is, this is not the natural state of affairs. Before the advent of agriculture women were either pregnant, and not cycling, or nursing, and not cycling. Menstrual cycling was an exception, not the rule. That may be why modern women, who lose more blood in menstruation over a lifetime than their ancestors ever did, are so prone to anaemia. How ironic it is that the contraceptive pill, which fools the body into thinking it is pregnant, is prescribed in such a way that it maintains this monthly rhythm, a practice that may be reassuring to modern women, but is distinctly unnatural. Roger Short, while he was at Edinburgh, started trials of a new system of giving oral contraceptives; he called it the tricycle pill, because it triggered menstruation once every three months rather than every month. It was not a great success, for psychological rather than physiological reasons.

So far we have looked at humans as sexually active animals, with their own special peculiarities. But there is a final peculiarity that concerns sexual inactivity. Human females go through a menopause, after which they are no longer capable of reproduction. But they do not die immediately. How did natural selection favour women who must, by the very act of staying alive, have competed with their own offspring? The answer, obviously, is that it was worth it to have a wise old woman around. Society depends on retaining and transmitting information from one generation to the next without using genes. One or two older individuals would be very valuable, remembering where water may be had in times of drought, how to cope with rare threats, looking after young ones, and so on, and the costs incurred by those elders would be more than outweighed by their value. But why should only *women* have stopped breeding? Perhaps women, certain that they have reproduced, can afford to give up; men are uncertain and keep trying. To suggest that older women would be unable to withstand the demands of raising another infant, whereas men do not have to suffer pregnancy, is to beg the question. Selection could surely just as easily have produced a woman who remained sturdy for all her days. Or could it? Why animals age is an enormous evolutionary problem that we simply cannot go into here, but the inevitability of aging might mean that women who did get pregnant at an advanced age would be more likely to succumb. If that were so then any woman who stopped being fertile would be more likely to stay alive and thus be better able to contribute the benefits of being around to assist her daughters and their daughters.

Men and women have many peculiarities as breeding animals, from the size and appearance of their sexual organs to the fact that they live beyond their reproductive span. These differences have long fascinated people, and all sorts of ideas have been advanced to account for them. We have tried to portray these fairly, and to show why in so many instances they do not hold water, generally because the thinkers insist on treating mankind as a special case. We are special, but for all except the most minuscule fraction of our past we were subject to the same kinds of forces as other animals. So any account of human peculiarities must make broad biological sense. That we cannot offer convincing accounts for some aspects of our breeding behaviour and apparatus is unfortunate, but probably reflects a paucity of the imagination. Someday we hope to know the answers.

So much of our nature is rooted in the differences between male and female that it is salutary to remember that we have not really uncovered a convincing reason for the continued existence of males. Human females have done a very good job of enlisting them into the struggle to reproduce, but who is to say that they might not be better off without us. Fortunately, an entirely new approach to the relevance of sex has suggested that we males might not, after all, be *completely* redundant.

SEX 'N' BUGS

Although the special role of sex explains much about human society and human evolution we are still left with many puzzles concerning exactly how and why sex evolved, and how and why it has remained valuable enough, in evolutionary terms, to have survived as long as it has. Perhaps the most powerful modern view of evolution is the idea of the selfish gene developed by William Hamilton and explored by researchers such as John Maynard Smith and Richard Dawkins. According to this theory, close relatives ought to co-operate with one another; by and large they do. And yet, in comparative terms we can see in human society that identical twins co-operate relatively little, while husband and wife co-operate a great deal. The reason, of course, is that husband and wife are together concerned with reproducing their genes, whereas identical twins are not (although, according to selfish genery, the identical twin of one of your parents ought to make a most loving and concerned uncle or aunt).

But this merely takes us back to the question of why sexual reproduction itself should be a good thing. The answer put forward in this book is that sex gains an evolutionary edge under conditions in which changes in the environment favour different combinations of genetic material. Sexual reproduction provides species with the ability to shuffle the genetic pack and come up with new combinations matched to the changing environment. So it is a group selected adaptation; groups with sex do better than groups without. But while it seems intuitively plausible that parents should vary the pioneers they are sending out into new environments, the mathematics do not work unless there are tens of thousands of progeny. The environment simply does not change quickly enough to make sex pay. A sexual species may, as in the case of the dandelion, give rise to asexual lines, clones, that do very well under a particular set of circumstances but die out when conditions change; provided that some members of the sexually reproducing variant still survive, this will not spell the end of the species.

The physical environment, variable though it may seem, is too stable to favour sex. But living things are also part of one another's environment, and one situation in which sex could be more or less continually an advantage would be when there is a constant war between food species and the species that prey on them. The predators try out new genetic combinations that may be more successful at overcoming the defences of the prey; the prey constantly need different defences to counter the different modes of attack of the predators. For example, some viruses, which are essentially predators on bacteria, recognise their prey, the bacteria, by a protein on the bacterial wall. That protein is encoded by a gene in the bacterium, and a mutant version might make a protein that the virus does not recognise, so for a while the mutant bacterium avoids attack. Then a mutation in the virus alters its recognition site and so the cycle begins again. Both evolve as fast as they can, and neither gains a decisive edge, in nature's equivalent of the arms race. Just to maintain its position in the ecology, a species has to evolve rapidly—a variant on the Red Queen hypothesis that we met earlier.[156]

Obviously, an individual that survives long enough to reproduce has succeeded, to some degree, in the environment in which it lives. Its offspring, however, may be faced with a slightly different environment, and so it may be worth shuffling the genetic pack even of a successful adult, which is where sex comes in. There is a conflict between the fitness of the individual here and now and the long-term success implicit in the flexibility of sexual reproduction. The extreme strategies that evolution has produced in response to this pressure lean very much towards one or the other of these conflicting requirements. Some species, for at least some of the time, go for all out reproduction of as many new individuals like the successful parent as possible. (The greenfly on your rose bush.) This provides for the most rapid increase in numbers under stable, albeit temporary, environmental conditions, and is called the r-strategy. The extreme alternative is to put care at a premium. This is advantageous if the ecological niche inhabited by the species is already full, so that offspring with a slight advantage over their neighbours will do best in the crowded world. The k-strategy, appropriate for conditions close to the limit of the carrying capacity of the environment for that species, often results in animals who bear few offspring that they carefully nurture (most birds, and of course our own species, are k-strategists). The Biblical seed, scattered on sand, stony ground and good soil, was produced by r-strategists.

You might expect, having paid attention to Williams' argument about pioneers, that r-strategists, sending masses of offspring out into a variable world, would make the offspring variable, by sex, but otherwise leave them to their own devices. And the k-strategists, secure in the very environment they have succeeded in, would make a few asexual clones. But that turns out to be untrue, and provides an insight into the true value of sex.

The idea of the two strategies for reproductive success has been around for nearly half a century, but for most of that time it was discussed almost solely in terms of competition for resources, or changes in the physical environment of the species. It was only in the 1970s that evolutionary theorists began to appreciate the impor- tance of other factors, including predation and the effects of disease—which are the same thing, really, since a pathogenic bacterium or virus can be thought of as a predator on the organism it invades. Donald Levin, of the University of Texas at Austin, is one of the pioneers of this new approach to an understanding of sex. Starting out with an investigation of the conditions under which plants choose different reproductive strategies, this work has now led to an improved understanding of the role of sexual reproduction in the evolutionary success of animals, including human animals.

The clearest example of the way predator pressures affect the reproductive strategies of plant species comes from a comparison of the tropical way of life with that of temperate regions. Plants do not, of course, nurture their offspring in quite the same way many animals do, but they still have an evolutionary choice between producing masses of offspring very similar to one another or a variety of offspring taking full advantage of sexual recombination. In the tropics, there are more insects and more browsing animals, both in terms of the number of species and the number of individ- uals. There is also more pressure from disease; more diseases attack tropical species than temperate species. So survival is harder for a tropical plant; if it is not eaten it will be attacked by disease. It is no coincidence, argues Levin, that tropical plants go for a version of the k-strategy for reproduction far more than their temperate counterparts do. Tropical flora favour the dioecious approach to sexual anatomy, with male and female flowers on separate plants so that there is no risk of self-fertilisation. In the tropics, flowers are far more likely to take full advantage of sex. From the Malayan rain forest, where 26 per cent of tree species are dioecious, to Costa Rica (22 per cent) and Hawaii (27 per cent) the picture is very much the same. Yet, by contrast, in the temperate latitudes it is far less likely that species will be dioecious. In southern California, the figure is only 3 per cent; in Australia 4 per cent; in Britain 3 per cent; and for all the seed plants of the world just 5 per cent.

In terms of geography, asexual reproduction among animals follows the same pattern. 'Parthenogenesis', says Levin, 'is almost exclusively restricted to temperate regions.'[157] But this is far from being the whole story. Many studies show that plants from the heartland of the range of a particular species have the greatest potential for genetic recombination—the greatest reluctance to combine their genes with close relations and the least prospect of self-fertilisation—while plants on the fringes of the species' range are more likely to lean towards an ability for self-fertilisation and reproductive compatibility with near genetic neighbours. This makes evolutionary sense, because out on the fringes of the species' range there may be few potential sexual partners to pick and choose from, so it is good strategy to be able to grab what is going. It also means that there is the greatest variability, including variability among the genes that provide resistance to pests and disease, in the interior of the species' range, the heartland where both plants and their pests have been evolving together in an environment which is physically well suited to carry large populations. Precisely in the region where there is least pressure from the physical environment we find most use of sexual recombination, a situation which would seem paradoxical without an understanding of the role of pests and disease. The pests need large host populations for their own success, and there are very subtle checks and balances which prevent a successful pest or pathogen from killing off all of its hosts and leaving itself with nowhere to live. All these factors help to explain why plant breeders seeking new genetic combinations to improve a species turn to plants from the centre of the species' range. That is where they find the qualities they are looking for. 'Open recombination would be immediately advantageous in the face of stringent, incessant and versatile pest pressure.'[158]

All this has interesting implications for plant breeders concerned with growing more food for a hungry world. In the great years of the 'green revolution' in the 1960s, it looked easy. Pests could be controlled by selecting a strain of plant resistant to a particular pathogen. But soon new, virulent strains of pathogen emerged, and the plant breeders had to counter by raiding the wild type of the plant species for a different combination of defensive genes, only to see the whole cycle repeat. Too great a reliance on individual varieties of major crops poses a very great risk to world agriculture; the more that plant breeders strive for an 'ideal' form of wheat, say, the more they are in effect producing a cloned variety without the variability necessary to respond rapidly to the changing pressures from pests. In nature, plants do not in general 'set' in one genetic pattern, or genome, in this way because of the variety of pressures on them.

You may have noticed something odd about this description of the war between plants and pathogens, however. Sex may be important in the evolutionary flexibility it gives the plants, but surely most of the pathogens—the bugs—are single-celled bacteria and viruses that do not generally use sex. How can they keep up their side of the arms race? It is a good point, but really this is expressing it the wrong way round. The single-celled organisms can evolve quickly because they reproduce quickly. Mutations may be rare in terms of generations, and it may take many generations, without the advantage of sex, for an advantageous mutation to become dominant. But there are so many generations each year (even each day or hour!) that the good news spreads very rapidly compared with the generation time of a large plant or an animal like ourselves. Indeed, the rapid generation time of the pathogens gives them such a huge advantage in the arms race that it is only thanks to sex and recombination that the large plants and large animals can fight back quickly enough to maintain, more or less, the status quo. And that is really the heart of the new understanding of the importance of sex in the animal world.

William Hamilton established the theme of this new approach in a landmark paper published in the journal *Oikos* in 1980.[159] And he explained his starting position very clearly for the audience at a Dahlem Conference in Berlin: 'A puzzle likely to occur to anyone hearing about evolution for the first time, and later very often forgotten, is that the rate of the whole process by natural selection must depend on the generation time. How, the listener then wonders, does anything manage to be as large and slow-breeding as an elephant? On the elephant's time scale of change, why do not bacteria of skin or gut, turning over generations a hundred thousand times faster, evolve almost instantly an ability to eat the vast body up?'[160] Hamilton then outlined the advantages for cells in getting together to form multicellular organisms, so-called metazoans. Assembled into a body, cells help to provide a mutual defence against predators, parasites, and the physical environment. The cells do this by working together to create a stable 'internal' environment. But the simple logistics of communicating among the members of a multicellular organism must slow down its growth rate, and therefore its reproductive rate. All parasites that remain much smaller than their host must, therefore, have an advantage in rate of evolution, an advantage which more than compensates for the gains the host has achieved by becoming multicellular. Suffering from evolutionary inertia and wide open to invasion, the multicellular organisms then needed a means to speed up their own evolution if they were to succeed. Sex provided that means. As Hamilton said, 'I believe that sex was the . . . invention that enabled metazoans and large plants to forge ahead against their handicaps of inertia and invasibility'.[161] It arises from the need that multicellular organisms have to identify their own cells and distinguish them from those of an invader. Such a system means that the cells of a body can co-operate with one another, and not with interlopers, and also that the full armoury of their defences can rapidly be brought to bear on any invading cells of a parasitic pathogen. Meanwhile, of course, the invaders are subject to intense selection pressure to disguise themselves as members of the body they are invading. As Hamilton puts it, 'an ongoing antagonistic co-evolution is to be expected over the matter of recognition.'[162]

The broad principles of such evolutionary competition are clear from the outset. The co-evolution will tend to produce the equivalent of 'passwords' associated with all the true cells of an organism. These would be simple chemical substances at first, just enough to let cells recognise one another. But as the invaders catch up, the pressure is on to evolve ever more elaborate passwords. An excellent system would be a set of complicated chemicals that change randomly from one generation to the next. Any parasite that had cracked the code would be thwarted as each new generation appeared. Sex and recombination provide an ideal way to create these passwords, and to recreate them in new, random combinations each generation. According to this line of argument, all the gross features of variation that are so obvious to us as the products of sexual reproduction may be merely incidental, part of the baggage of recombination but actually serving very little evolutionary role, with all the action taking place at the cellular level.

Hamilton and others have developed mathematical models which attempt to calculate the extent of the advantage sex confers in this battle against invaders. In these models the greatest advantage comes when the password is made up of several syllables that can be swapped about and rearranged. This is exactly what happens in nature. The recognition molecules, as we will see a little later, are made up of different regions, each encoded by a different stretch of DNA. The different genes combine to code for the password. Sex and recombination move these syllabic regions about to create entirely new chemical passwords.

In the particular models used by Hamilton the sexual species remains at an advantage provided each pair of parents produces, on average, fourteen or more offspring. The exact number is not important; what is important is that this is a biologically plausible number. Even human beings, who are extreme examples of k-strategists, might be able to manage this sort of level of reproduction. The earlier studies, not taking account of all the subtleties in Hamilton's model, found that the two-fold genetic advantage of asexual reproduction could only be overcome by the advantages of sex if the numbers of competing offspring were much larger, many thousands per breeding pair. That was fine in the early days of life, when rapid exploitation of the environment was the name of the game. But it was no good for much of history, indeed probably not since the development of animals much more complicated than sponges. Hamilton's work shows that sex could have been advantageous for our immediate ancestors. It also shows, of course, that in the traditional family unit of the developed world, with just a couple of children, the advantage of sex over asexual reproduction has already been lost, especially when the father offers little parental care.

Hamilton's mathematical models show that extensive amounts

of recombination are essential in fluctuating environments if the environment directly affects the way cells learn to develop new passwords. 'As selection intensity increases there comes a point, usually achievable at moderate levels of fecundity, where a sexual species has an advantage over any asexual strain even when the latter are given a two-fold advantage in effective fecundity. Asexuals then die out or are maintained only at very low frequency . . . high levels of recombination facilitate such exclusion of asexuals by sexuals.'[163] The real point is that, by treating bacteria and other predators as the environment, Hamilton has discovered an environment that changes rapidly enough to make sex pay. By the time a long-lived host is ready to reproduce, its rapidly multiplying pathogens will in all likelihood have evolved the ability to attack it. Under those circumstances, the *worst* thing the host could do would be to produce an identical copy of itself, ready to be pounced upon by the parasite. Sex, and an offspring different enough to thwart the parasites, is essential.

This new perspective on the evolutionary significance of sex takes us far away from the world of animal behaviour and speculation about the peacock's tail. It starts from the very reasonable assumption that the single most important thing for the cells in a multicelled organism to be able to do is to recognise the other cells in the body, and to distinguish friends, who share your genes, from foes, who do not. Identifying friend and foe involves what is called the immune reaction, the most sophisticated molecular recognition system that has evolved. Molecular biologists probing the mysteries of self-recognition in vertebrates—including mankind—have paid particular attention to a group called the histocompatibility antigens (part of the major histocompatibility complex, or MHC). These antigens are the passwords, the identification markers which the body's defence mechanisms recognise as 'self'. It is the absence of the correct histocompatibility antigens, or the presence of incorrect antigens, which triggers the body into mustering its defences and attacking an invader.

It seems very likely that these identification labels have evolved out of the first recognition system that the earliest multi-celled life forms must have had in order to exist at all as co-operative assemblages of cells. But in spite of their profound importance to an understanding of evolution and, it now turns out, sex, the histocompatibility antigens have been the subject of intense study in recent years for quite another reason. Any mechanism by which the body recognises foreign cells as invaders, and is triggered to attack them, is of profound importance to the medical problems of organ transplants and tissue rejection. And this is the context in which Jean Dausset, Professor of Experimental Medicine in the College of France, did research on antigens in man, research that led in 1980 to the award of the Nobel Prize in Physiology and Medicine, jointly with Baruj Benacerraf and George Snell.

Almost every cell in your body is identified not by one password but by three, three different histocompatibility antigens which are known in the trade as A, B and C. The cells that read this information are the white blood cells, or T-lymphocytes, and although the details of how they recognise the MHC molecules remains a mystery, their reaction to the labels is very clear. Cells without the correct combination of A, B and C codes to identify them are immediately and violently attacked by a particular brand of T-lymphocytes called killer cells, more properly known as cyto-toxic T-cells, from the Greek, and they literally kill cells. It is their uncompromising response to invaders that causes grafted tissues to be rejected and makes the life of the transplant surgeon so difficult. If there were just a few versions of the A, B and C molecules, the surgeon's life would be much easier, since there would be a good chance of finding a donor whose tissues carried the same identification labels. But in fact each of the three antigens comes in about 40 different varieties, an extremely high level of polymorphism. The likelihood of finding a donor whose tissues have exactly the same combination of three antigens out of all the possible permutations is very small. It is because they share genes, including the MHC genes, that there is a much better chance of an approximate match in the tissues of near relatives. That is why siblings are sometimes called upon to supply some bone marrow or even a kidney for an ailing brother or sister.

The histocompatibility antigens have clearly been selected by evolutionary pressures to minimise the likelihood that two bodies of creatures even in the same species will carry identical passwords on their cells. The pressure, which goes back to the beginnings of multicellular life, was presumably to prevent one collection of cells from taking over another. The result today is that an invading pathogen doesn't just have the task of identifying, and mimicking, one password with which it can gain admittance to all the individual members of a species; it has the far harder task of cracking a different combination of passwords every time it invades a new individual. This may very well be the key advantage that sexual reproduction has over asexual reproduction in the Darwinian struggle for survival.

As Dausset said in his Nobel address, the antigens must be important because they are so ubiquitous, 'being present at the surface of all (or almost all) cells of the organism. This suggests that they play a *very general* biological role.'[164] As Dausset further explained, 'without self-recognition, each specialised cell and each tissue would be isolated and incapable of surviving . . . self-recognition is an active phenomenon.'[165] This activity extends to the evolutionary level. The more effectively a bacterium or virus evolves its disguise, the more pressure there is on the host to refine its recognition codes; the better the cytotoxic T-cells become at detecting invaders, the more pressure there is on the invaders to perfect their disguises. By the time molecular biologists had the tools and techniques to investigate the genes that control the production of the histocompatibility antigens, they fully expected to find evidence of rapid evolution and diversification. But the extent of their findings ran far beyond those expectations.[166]

The A, B and C antigens together are just one aspect of a larger and more complex immune system. This includes two other kinds of lymphocytes as well as the cytotoxic T-cells, and another group of antigens called Class II (the A, B and C group being Class I). Class II antigens appear only on certain cells, and are signals to the other kinds of T-lymphocytes, called 'helper' and 'suppressor' cells. As their names suggest, these cells are involved in deciding how strongly the body responds to an invader (helper) and whether the cytotoxic T-cells are brought into action at all (suppressor). The interactions are complex and are only beginning to be understood; what matters here, though, is that like the Class I antigens those in Class II are involved in identifying and responding to foreign cells, and they too are highly polymorphic.

Using the traditional techniques of immunology and the more modern tricks of genetic engineering, biologists have been able to map the entire major histocompatibility complex, the group of genes responsible for the production of Class I and Class II antigens. The big surprise came when a team under Leroy Hood, at CalTech, used radioactive atoms inserted into cloned copies of the MHC genes to look for the genes that coded for the production of the histocompatibility antigens. The study was carried out on the genetic material of a familiar strain of laboratory mouse, the Balb/c, and the team expected the technique to pick up about eight genes— three or four that coded for the histocompatibility antigens, and another three or four that actually coded for a slightly different antigen associated with lymphocytes, but which differed from the histocompatibility antigen genes too subtly for the test to tell the difference. To their astonishment, they actually found no less than 36 genes coding for Class I antigens in the Balb/c mouse.[167]

More studies, by Hood's team and others, showed that mouse, human and pig genetic material all show the same pattern. By chance, the particular mouse MHC material that was the first to be cloned is also the most complicated, but all the others have at least 20 genes for the comparable part of the MHC, which is still more than twice as many as the organism needs in order to manufacture the few variations on the Class I themes that it actually uses. What on Earth could the extra genes be for?

The answer provided a completely new insight into one aspect of evolution. Molecular biologists had already come across cases of extra copies of genes, found first in the group of genes that code for haemoglobin, the oxygen-carrying pigment molecule of red blood cells. It seemed at first as if these so-called pseudogenes were simply pieces of genetic junk, copies or partial copies of real genes that were manufactured by mistake during the reproductive process. This could have occurred at any stage in evolutionary history, and the extra copies have since been handed on willy nilly from generation to generation by the mindless DNA copying process. These accidental, slightly mutated duplicates of working genes are useless because they are no longer capable of passing on their genetic message and ordering the production of proteins by the cell. Such an explanation might account for the occasional pseudogene found in the complex coding for haemoglobin or other families of genes. But it takes a lot of swallowing to believe that more than half of the genetic material in the MHC is actually genetic junk that cannot be got rid of. The possession of so many pseudogenes suggests, rather, that they continue to exist because they provide some kind of evolutionary advantage. And that advantage could very well be that they provide the basis for the remarkable polymorphism of the proteins which are manufactured by the MHC and become the histocompatibility antigens. Even more important, they provide the means by which the passwords on the antigen code can be changed, to the confusion of invading pathogens.

The evidence comes from investigations of the way mutations arise in the MHC complex of mice—evidence that shows that the Class I genes can communicate by swapping chunks of DNA with one another. Molecular biologists were put on the track of this phenomenon by the discovery that the same mutation could turn up independently in different mice. This should have been exceedingly, almost undetectably, rare, but was in fact quite common. When the DNA of the mutant genes involved was cloned and mapped in detail, researchers discovered that the puzzling mutation did not consist of a simple point mutation, changing one letter of the genetic code. Instead a whole chunk of DNA had changed, and this section corresponded exactly with a section in a *different* Class I gene. The DNA appeared to have jumped from one place on the chromosome to another, and with hindsight, it is easy to see how this might occur. During meiosis, when crossing over takes place, there might be a misalignment between the pair of chromosomes. A gene could be joined on to a neighbour on the opposite chromosome, rather than to its own partner. In itself this creation of variety by misalignment does not require pseudogenes. The advantage of pseudogenes, it has been argued, is that they allow mutations to occur in stretches of DNA that are not being used, and these are then restored to functioning by other alterations to the genome.

Misalignments are not the only way to exchange portions of DNA; swaps could also occur through an error in the 'proof reading' mechanisms that check each copy as it is made.

The proofreading enzymes can snip out mistakes from the newly copied DNA chain and splice in a good version of the offending stretch of material taken from the original. If, in the course of their proofreading, they make the mistake of comparing a section of DNA not with its original but with the gene next door to the original, then they will busily snip out a perfectly good chunk of

DNA and splice in a copy of part of the wrong gene. The process, dubbed gene conversion, only happens with near neighbours, and the close grouping of genes in the MHC makes it a very likely site for such activity. By such processes, working genes may be altered dramatically by the inclusion of chunks of material from non-functioning pseudogenes, and pseudogenes themselves may be restored to working order if the mutations which disable them are replaced by working parts from another gene. The whole MHC becomes a hotbed of mutation, with information being exchanged among a family of closely related genes.

The advantages are obvious. It enables the organism to keep one step ahead of invaders changing the immune passwords. Mutations can occur frequently, and in complex, unpredictable ways that make for great variety. None of this, however, would be possible if it were not for sex, because all of the crosstalk among the genes occurs as a by-product of sexual reproduction, with its crossing over and recombination.

There is, however, still another twist to the tale of histocompatibility antigens, transplant rejection, sex, and the ability to detect invading cells in the body. On one occasion during the life cycle of a sexually reproducing species it is absolutely essential to accept a foreign cell and not fight it but work with it—during reproduction. Strictly speaking, this lowering of the defences must happen twice in mammalian reproduction. First, the egg must accept the sperm, with its different histocompatibility antigens. Then the mother must not only accept but nurture the resulting fertilised egg. She has to accept and succour one particular invader while retaining her ability to destroy pathogens.

The fetus has been described as 'nature's transplant'. It already has its own antigens and its own self-recognition codes—it must have, since the whole point of sexual reproduction, we now see, is to give the offspring a different set of codes that will ensure its resistance to disease. And yet it grows within the mother. Inevitably there is a fine balance between the mechanisms in the mother's blood which automatically repel the invader and other mechanisms, more recently evolved, that suppress the immune reaction in this special case. Just how delicate the balance is we can see from the fact that three-quarters of all fertilised eggs fail to come to term in human mothers.[168] Some—perhaps the majority—of these losses must be the result of an adverse interaction between the histocompatibility antigens brought together in the egg by the sex cells from the two parents.

Clearly, it is best for a prospective parent to choose a partner with compatible antigens and the best likelihood of producing a viable fertilised egg that comes to term. There is a considerable body of evidence that in many species the cues which trigger the appropriate response (acceptance or rejection of a suitor) depend on scent, and that odour carries information about the passwords of identity present on an individual's cells. Pregnant mice and wild horses will absorb their fetuses back into their bodies and become sexually receptive once again when presented with an unrelated male, and the resorption occurs in mice even when they are exposed only to the smell of the strange male's urine. Inbred strains of mice that differ from each other only in the genes of the MHC complex have now been produced, and mice from one such strain can be trained to choose one branch of a maze, distinguished from other branches only by a trace of urine from mice with a different MHC, instead of urine from their own strain. These subtle experiments establish that by smell alone mice, at least, can identify whether or not other mice have similar histocompatibility antigens to themselves.

But now comes the twist. You might expect that it would be easier to persuade the mother's body to accept the fetus if the father has similar histocompatibility antigens to herself. The resulting fetus would be less like an invader and more like her. But if sex is a good thing in evolutionary terms, then the most successful individuals—those which produce most descendants—ought to be the ones that mate with individuals different from themselves. Sure enough, as we have seen, in most species individuals avoid matings with close kin. Wild mice, for example, do not pair with their litter mates even though these are often the nearest and otherwise most accessible potential partners. There is no mystery about this. In the past, individuals that lacked this discrimination did mate with their close relatives, and by losing the advantages of sex their descendants have failed to survive; the survivors, the individuals around today, are descended from lines with a preference for outbreeding, and this, it now seems, means individuals that choose partners with different histocompatibility antigens.

People, though, may be an exception today. We live in unnatural surroundings, bathe frequently and drench ourselves in smells that have nothing to do with our histocompatibility antigens. It makes no difference whether the smells are perfumes intended to enhance our appeal to others, or unpleasant reminders of tobacco and alcoholic drink. The effect is the same, to reduce the effectiveness of our natural ability to select as sexual partners other individuals most likely to combine with ourselves to produce viable offspring. We choose our partners for other reasons—intellectual compatibility, a sense of humour, good looks, money or whatever—which may be fine in their way but which don't tell us anything about the likelihood of the partnership producing children. In many cases that is not important; in many others, would-be parents are frustrated by their inability to conceive a child together, or for the mother to carry it to term. In a classic test reported in 1981, three women who had suffered several spontaneous abortions were each found to share many histocompatibility antigens with their respective husbands. Doctors advising the couples treated each of the women, when pregnant, with a cocktail of foreign lymphocytes, calculated to produce a strong immune response. In every case, the mother produced a healthy baby. Quite clearly, the cell-surface antigens help to promote outbreeding by making inbred fetuses less viable. And this in turn feeds back directly into the MHC, because the outbreeding itself increases the polymorphism which is now seen as a key weapon in the body's fight against invasion and disease. Unromantic though it may seem, the phenomenon of love at first sight may simply be the powerful response of the body to the scent of a very different set of histocompatibility antigens. (Could there be a great untapped potential for some unscrupulous biochemist to manufacture a true aphrodisiac, love potions tailored to attract particular individuals by taking their MHC into account?)

It is not just sex, but the combination of sex and polymorphism, that gives a sexually reproducing species an edge in the evolutionary struggle. Although bacteria can and do exchange DNA, they lack the extreme degree of polymorphism that enables multi-celled organisms like ourselves to keep up in the biological arms race. In plants, fruitflies, mice and men between 30 per cent and 40 per cent of all genetic loci are polymorphic, even though selection ought to weed out the less fit variations on the theme very effectively. This variability used to be cause for concern to diehard evolutionists, but it makes sense seen as a defence against predators. The potential for variety is truely astonishing. Ten genetic loci which each correlated with 50 alleles—in round terms the sort of variability in the MHC of mouse and man—would provide 50^{10} combinations, 10^{17} variations on the theme. That is a hundred million million combinations. Bring in the prospect of recombination with a similarly endowed partner, and the number is squared, to 10^{34}. How can we put such an astronomical number in perspective? The number of atoms of carbon in a 60 carat diamond (the Koh-I-Noor weighs 109 carats) is about 6×10^{23}. The number of potential variations on the biological theme corresponding to our hypothetical, but realistic, example is ten thousand million times greater than this. Something encourages the survival of variety *per se*, and that something is the threat of invasion by pathogens. This applies to plants as much as to animals, and although vertebrates in general and mammals in particular provide the most intriguing case studies for us as human beings, it is in many ways easier to work with plants and to identify how they resist invasion.

Hans Bremermann, of the University of California at Berkeley, reported just such a study in 1980.[169] He identified self-incompatibility loci in flowering plants (angiosperms) which carry out a similar function in plants to the role of the MHC in man; they decide which sex cells (pollen) are acceptable partners with which to form fertilised seeds. As Bremermann points out, in plants as in people a reluctance to combine in the production of offspring with closely similar individuals favours rare alleles and acts against the most common versions of a particular gene. This is an effective means of promoting polymorphism. On this picture, it is hardly surprising that when agricultural practices reduce the polymorphism of a strain it becomes susceptible to disease. The Irish potato famine of the nineteenth century is the classic example; but there are repeated failures of cereal grain varieties and other crops today. Ironically, such failure may be as bad for the parasites as for the crop, since it leaves them with little to parasitise.

The host plant does best if it is not infected by parasites, but the parasite will do best if there are many hosts to attack. Because the parasites' attack inevitably reduces the fitness of the host, in evolutionary terms the parasite is faced with conflicting objectives, and has to strike the right balance to ensure its own survival. When we interfere with nature by choosing only the 'best' plants and breeding them up for our farms, we upset this natural balance. We remove the defences that the parasites have evolved, over many millions of generations, to attack just some varieties and then only with just enough strength for their own good. Many alleles are required if the associated polymorphism is to be a barrier against disease, says Bremermann, and he cites the astronomical numbers for the amount of possible variability as evidence of the same mechanism at work in plants as in mammals.

Parasites can thus do well if there are sub-populations adapted to attack different hosts. But the host, both because it is variable and because its immune system can, given time, defend it against new invaders, is not always vanquished. Bremermann cites the history of influenza outbreaks as an example of a pathogen that itself evolves rapidly and briefly causes havoc among the human population, but which on every occasion is quickly countered by the skill of human defence mechanisms in learning to identify the new surface code words evolved by the flu virus. The flu outbreak after World War I killed more people than the war, to be sure, but the survivors had immune systems that could cope with the new flu threat.

But the adaptability of the immune system depends on it having plenty of variety to play with. In plants the loss of the variability stored in the natural gene pool could be a real threat to plant breeders trying to keep one step ahead of the very rapid evolution enjoyed by parasites such as the fungi that cause rusts in wheat, barley and oats. Over the years the plant breeders have repeatedly developed strains of these cereal crops resistant to rust, and repeatedly they have seen rust coming back after several years of cultivation. Each time this happens a new cereal strain has to be developed. The breeders take in slightly different genetic material from the older varieties, which retain much more polymorphism than the new, high yield crops, and give those crops extra resistance and another short lease of life. As yet, however, the plant breeders do not seem to have recognised, or put to practical use, the discovery that it is *the polymorphism itself* that provides the major protection to plants in the wild. A unique set of genes might provide excellent resistance to a particular suite of disease organisms, but because the pathogens can change so much more quickly than their host they can evolve a way through the defences. The protection doesn't last. It is sex, and variability, that make for a truly hardy variety.

The new view of sex and evolution is a surprising one, and yet it does make sense. It also represents yet another blow to the egocentric way in which we tend to view the world. Once we thought that Man ruled an Earth that sat at the centre of the Universe. Then the Earth was relegated to the orbit of an ordinary star that was itself just a speck in one of many billions of galaxies. Mankind was not important either, simply the expression of one set of tactics adopted by a collection of DNA molecules to get themselves copied at the expense of other collections of DNA molecules. That much we can cope with. And we could still look upon our own, and other animals', tactics with wonder and curiosity. Now, to quote William Hamilton, 'some of the most spectacular variation of animals, as between males and females in polygynous species . . . will appear at least partly as an epiphenomenon of the cryptic variation in enzymes, antigens, and other proteins'.[170] Sex, it seems, is a defence mechanism. Mixing two sets of DNA in one body protects it from predators. All the rest is icing on the cake.

EPILOGUE

THE SOLUTION

We began by asking why women bothered to have sons. What evolutionary advantage could possibly compensate for the loss of half your reproductive potential? The traditional answer sees sex as a means of promoting variety. When a successful animal or plant has exhausted its own patch it must, if its genes are to continue, send out pioneers to explore new lands. If those lands are likely to be slightly different from the homeland then the parent can do better if it uses sexual reproduction to combine its lot with another parent and sends out very variable offspring. That way at least one of the offspring has the chance of being the pioneer best suited to the patch in which it lands.

The trouble with this story is that, for the vast majority of species alive today, it simply will not work. If sex is to have the edge, then either the environment must change more quickly than it does, or the offspring sent out must number in the hundreds of thousands. That was probably fine in the early days of life, and it may still be fine for elms, aphids and oysters, but it is of no relevance to ourselves. Why then is sex so prevalent? We don't know for sure, but it may simply be because a species that reproduces sexually exists longer and so is more likely to give rise to new species than is an asexual cloning species. Members of the clone reproduce more quickly than their sexual relatives, but when the environment changes they are trapped. The sexual species can split into new species. So most of the species we see use sex, and sexual reproduction may be the one phenomenon best explained by the otherwise discredited notion of group selection.

Another possibility, which may be operating in addition to the argument we have just outlined, is that organisms today cannot get out of sex. The modifications to the cellular machinery that were necessary to ensure regular and smooth meiosis and fusion were many and complex, and are not easily reversed. As a result many species are stuck with sex. Many asexual species continue to produce male and female sex cells, but rather than combining sex cells from different individuals they self-fertilise. Such a process is effectively cloning. And some of the vertebrates that have become asexual still need to find a male willing to provide a sperm, not for the genes it carries but as a trigger to start the egg developing.

In this traditional view, sex is something we, in common with most animals and plants, cannot get out of, much though it might profit us to do so. Evolution cannot run backwards. Sex nevertheless explains a great deal of what we see around us. Female and male genders seem to be all but inevitable. Females gain an evolutionary edge by channelling a little more investment into their offspring. Males have other goals. They win by finding a greater number of exploitable females to bear their offspring. Much of animal behaviour can be understood in these terms. Of course there are also nurturant males and competitive females, but these are exceptional and often reveal that the whole suite of behaviours that we recognise as female goes along with taking care of the young, while maleness goes along with competing for mates. There is a clear conflict of interest between the sexes. Females originally got little, bar the genes, out of males and have adopted a host of tactics to obtain more investment from their partner. Getting a male to contribute parental care is one solution. Males wanted nothing but mates, and likewise have adopted a variety of means to obtain as many partners as possible. But both genders can compromise if that is what it takes to increase their reproductive success. One might think that the female, having control over reproduction, would be able to mutate so as to do away with her reliance on the selfish male parasite. That we males continue to exist suggests that, in the battle of the sexes, males have been victorious.

So much is certainly true in the animal world; the human case is more contentious. Males, we have said, continue to exist because the reproductive machinery requires a sperm to get it going. But this is not so. Doctors working on test-tube fertilisation have discovered, much to their surprise, that human eggs, all on their own and with no help from a sperm, can divide. It requires no great leap of imagination to see that in the very near future women might be quite capable of dispensing with men altogether. The technology of test-tube babies already exists, and if an adequately supported team were to put their minds to the problem it would be no time before women could do without men entirely. They would be able to clone themselves. Admittedly they would be reliant on technology to do so, but mankind is already entirely reliant on technology to survive. A dependancy on machinery for reproduction would not be that great an extra burden. Human males, stripped of their parental care, are truly redundant.

Or are we? If sex exists because it enables organisms to mount an effective defence against pathogens, as we think it does, then males are not useless. They are needed to ensure that children have a different set of biochemical identity markers from their parents. Perhaps we have at last identified the true role of males in the human species. Sex and drugs fulfil the same purpose. Our job is to provide the means by which females can fight off disease. But our relief, as males, may be shortlived, because just as we have found in the course of our investigation that all the other possible roles for the human male have been rendered redundant by the development of a civilised way of life, so too, perhaps, has this role nearly outlived its time. In the developed world at least, diseases are countered today by medical means; one at least, smallpox, has been eradicated from the face of the Earth. Genetic engineering makes it increasingly likely that in future medical science will be even better equipped to cope with the invading pathogens that threaten the human species with disease. Women who could clone themselves could presumably also find better technological weapons against disease, and these might render the awesome complexity of the immune system irrelevant.

But we must put in a word of warning in our favour. The example of the farmers' battle against rust should be taken as a cautionary tale, an indication that we men may not yet have quite outlasted our evolutionary usefulness to humans. The image we put forward earlier, of a world inhabited by parthenogenetically reproducing females, would depend crucially on the ability of doctors and molecular biologists to keep disease in check. One slip could wreak havoc. It would be as well to retain men and the ability to make use of them.

Men may be redundant, but most women probably don't object too much. A small minority might like to do away with men completely. It is a theme that pervades the more extreme feminist propaganda, though few go as far as Cheryl, a character in a recent novel. She 'wrote terrifyingly ferocious pamphlets from the

Crouch End Women's Collective calling for the extermination of men and the abortion of male foetuses'.[171] The truly terrifying thing is that it could happen. The technology of asexual female reproduction in the human species really isn't that far off. If suitably dedicated women overcame any ethical objections and applied themselves to the task they could be cloned within a decade. But they have not done so yet, and we men are not yet completely useless. Until technology catches up with their hopes, if it ever does, we have the perfect answer to those women who see males for what they are, biological parasites on the parental care of females: if it weren't for men, you would all be riddled with disease.

REFERENCES

1 Attenborough, D., 1980, *Life on Earth: A Natural History*, 1981, Little, Brown: Boston. This is an excellent overview of the history of life.
2 We do discuss the mechanics of DNA in more detail in our previous book: Gribbin, J. and Cherfas, J., 1982, *The Monkey Puzzle: Reshaping the Evolutionary Tree*, Pantheon: New York.
3 *The Oxford Dictionary of Quotations*, 3rd edition, 1979, Oxford University Press: Oxford. p. 118.
4 Margulis, L., 1981, *Symbiosis in Cell Evolution: Life and its Environment on the Early Earth*, Freeman: San Francisco.
5 Lewin, R. A., 1982, 'Microbial galley slaves', *Nature*, 300: 479–480.
6 Harrison, E. R., 1981, *Cosmology*, Cambridge University Press: Cambridge. p. 337.
7 Dawkins, R., 1976, *The Selfish Gene*, Oxford University Press: Oxford. pp. 30–32.
8 Williams, G. C., 1975, *Sex and Evolution*, Princeton University Press: Princeton, New Jersey.
9 Maynard Smith, J., 1978, *The Evolution of Sex*, Cambridge University Press: Cambridge. p. 54.
10 McWhirter, N., 1983, *Guinness Book of Records* 1984 Edition, Sterling: New York. p. 16.
11 As note 8, p. 102.
12 Carson, H. L., 1967, "Selection for parthenogenesis in *Drosophila mercatorum*', *Genetics*, 55: 157–171.
13 Olsen, M. W., 1965, 'Twelve year summary of selection for parthenogenesis in Beltsville Small White turkeys', *British Poultry Science*, 6:1–6.
14 As note 8, p. 105.
15 Daly, M., and Wilson, M., 1978, *Sex, Evolution, and Behavior*, Duxbury Press: Reading, Massachusetts. p. 46.
16 As note 8, p. 109.
17 As note 8, p. 147.
18 As note 8, p. 158.
19 As note 9, pp. 33 *et seq.*
20 As note 9, p. 36.

REFERENCES

21 Gardner, M., 1970, *The Annotated Alice*, Penguin: New York. p. 210.

22 As note 9, p. 26.

23 As note 15, p. 47.

24 Hoyle, F., 1960, *The Black Cloud*, Penguin: New York.

25 Jacob, F., 1982, *The Possible and the Actual*, Pantheon: New York.

26 Explored in more detail in Chapter 5, see notes 94 and 95 below.

27 McMillen, M. M., 1979, 'Differential mortality by sex in fetal and neonatal deaths', *Science*, 204: 89–91.

28 Hutt, C., 1972, *Males and Females*, Penguin: New York. p. 23.

29 Cited in Daly and Wilson (note 15). p. 75.

30 As note 4.

31 Shu, F., 1982, *The Physical Universe*, University Science Books: Mill Valley, California. p. 539.

32 Parker, G. A., Baker, R. R. and Smith, V. G. F., 1972, 'The origin and evolution of gamete dimorphism and the male-female phenomenon', *Journal of Theoretical Biology*, 36: 529–553.

33 As note 15, p. 51.

34 Marx, G., 1978, *The Groucho Letters*, Woodhill: New York. p. 91.

35 Haldeman, J., 1976, *The Forever War*, Ballantine: New York.

36 Emlen, S. T., 1981, 'The ornithological roots of sociobiology', *Auk*, 98: 400–403.

37 As note 7.

38 Bertram, B., 1978, *Pride of Lions*, J. M. Dent: London.

39 Ridley, M., 1978, 'Paternal care', *Animal Behaviour*, 26: 904–932.

40 Emlen, S. T. and Oring, L. W., 1977, 'Ecology, sexual selection and the evolution of mating systems', *Science*, 197: 215–223.

41 Woolfenden, G. E., 1975, 'Florida scrub jay helpers at the nest', *Auk*, 92: 1–15.

42 Coulson, J. C. and Thomas, C. S., 1983, 'Mate choice in the kittiwake gull', in P. Bateson, ed., *Mate Choice*, Cambridge University Press, Cambridge. pp. 361–376.

43 LeBoeuf, B. J. and Peterson, R. S., 1969, 'Social status and mating activity in elephant seals', *Science*, 163: 91–93. LeBoeuf, B. J., 1974, 'Male-male competition and reproductive success in elephant seals', *American Zoologist*, 14: 163–176.

44 Orians, G. H., 1969, 'On the evolution of mating systems in birds and mammals', *American Naturalist*, 103: 589–603. Verner, J., and Willson, M. F., 1966, 'The influence of habitats on mating systems of North American passerine birds', *Ecology*, 47: 143–147.

45 Cronin, E. W., Jr. and Sherman, P. W., 1977, 'A resource-based mating system: the orange-rumped honeyguide', *Living Bird*, 15: 5–32.

46 Clutton-Brock, T., Guinness, F. E. and Albon, S. D., 1982, *Red Deer: Behavior and Ecology of Two Sexes*, University of Chicago Press: Chicago.

47 Hogan-Warburg, L., 1966, 'Social behavior of the ruff, *Philomachus pugnax* (L.)', *Ardea*, 54: 109–229.

48 Hausfater, G., 1975, *Dominance and Reproduction in Baboons* (Papio cynocephalus): *A Quantitative Analysis*, S. Karger: New York.

49 Davies, N. B., 1983, 'Polyandry, cloaca-pecking and sperm competition in dunnocks', *Nature*, 302: 334–336.

50 Jenni, D. A. and Collier, G., 1972, 'Polyandry in the American jacana (*Jacana spinosa*)', *Auk*, 89: 743–765.

51 Ridpath, M. G., 1972, 'The Tasmanian native hen, *Tribonyx mortierii*', CSIRO Wildlife Research, 17: 1–118.

52 Partridge, L., 1980, 'Mate choice increases a component of offspring fitness in fruit flies', *Nature*, 283: 290–291.

53 Petrie, M., 1983, 'Female moorhens compete for small fat males', *Science*, 220: 413–415.

54 Nisbet, I. C. T., 1973, 'Courtship-feeding, egg-size and breeding success in common terns', *Nature*, 241: 141–142.

55 LeBoeuf, B. J., Whiting, R. J. and Gault, R. F., 1972, 'Perinatal behaviour of nothern elephant seals and their young', *Behaviour*, 43: 121–156.

56 Fisher, R. A., 1930, *The Genetical Theory of Natural Selection*, Oxford University Press: Oxford.

57 Andersson, M., 1982, 'Female choice selects for extreme tail length in a widowbird', *Nature*, 299: 818–820.

58 Cited by Halliday, T., 1980, *Sexual Strategy*, Oxford University Press: Oxford. pp. 68–69.

59 Beecher, M. D. and Beecher, I. M., 1979, 'Sociobiology of bank swallows: reproductive strategy of the male', *Science*, 205: 1282–1285.

60 Barash, D. P., 1976, 'Male response to apparent female adultery in the mountain bluebird (*Sialia currucoides*): an evolutionary interpretation', *American Naturalist*, 110: 1097–1101.

61 Gowaty, P. A., 1981, 'Aggression of breeding eastern bluebirds (*Sialia sialis*) toward their mates and models of intra- and interspecific intruders', *Animal Behaviour*, 29: 1013–1027.

62 Atalo, R. V., Lundberg, A. and Stahlbrandt, K., 1982, 'Why do pied flycatcher females mate with already-mated males?' *Animal Behaviour*, 30: 585–593.

63 Thornhill, R., 1976, 'Sexual selection and nuptial feeding behavior in *Bittacus apicalis* (Insecta: Mecoptera)', *American Naturalist*, 110: 529–548.

REFERENCES

64 Zenone, P. G., Sims, M. E. and Erickson, C. J., 1979, 'Male ring dove behavior and the defense of genetic paternity', *American Naturalist*, 114: 615–626.

65 Bray, O. E., Kenelly, J. J. and Guarino, J. L., 1975, 'Fertility of eggs produced on territories of vasectomized red-winged blackbirds', *Wilson Bulletin*, 87: 187–195.

66 As note 56.

67 As note 3, p. 360.

68 Mrosovsky, N. and Yntema, C. L., 1980, 'Temperature dependence of sexual differentiation in sea turtles: implications for conservation practices', *Biological Conservation*, 18: 271–280.

69 Ferguson, M. W. J. and Joanen, T., 1983, 'Temperature-dependent sex determination in *Alligator mississippiensis*', *Journal of Zoology*, 200: 143–177.

70 Leutert, R., 1975, 'Sex-determination in *Bonellia*', in R. Reinboth, ed., *Intersexuality in the Animal Kingdom*, Springer-Verlag: New York.

71 Quoted without source by Hapgood, F., 1979, *Why Males Exist: An Inquiry Into the Evolution of Sex*, Mentor NEL: New York. p. 69.

72 Fischer, E. A., 1980, 'The relationship between mating system and simultaneous hermaphroditism in the coral reef fish, *Hypoplectus nigricans* (Serranidae)', *Animal Behaviour*, 28: 620–633.

73 Daly, M. and Wilson, M., 1983, *Sex, Evolution, and Behavior*, 2nd ed., Willard Grant Press: Boston, Massachusetts. p. 240.

74 Hamilton, W. D., 1964, 'The genetical evolution of social behaviour', I & II, *Journal of Theoretical Biology*, 7: 1–52.

75 Trivers, R. L. and Hare, H., 1976, 'Haplodiploidy and the evolution of the social insects', *Science*, 191: 249–263.

76 Metcalf, R. A., 1980, 'Sex ratios, parent-offspring conflict, and local competition for mates in the social wasps *Polistes metricus* and *Polistes variatus*', *American Naturalist*, 116: 642–654. Noonan, K. M., 1978, 'Sex ratio of parental investment in colonies of the social wasp *Polistes fuscipes*', *Science*, 199: 1354–1356.

77 Hamilton, W. D., 1967, 'Extraordinary sex ratios', *Science*, 165: 477–488.

78 Wylie, H. G., 1966, 'Some mechanisms that affect the sex ratio of *Nasonia vitripennes* (Walk.) (Hymenoptera: Pteromalidae) reared from superparasitized housefly pupae', *Canadian Entomologist*, 98: 645–653.

79 Walker, I., 1967, 'Effect of population density on the viability and fecundity in *Nasonia vitripennis* Walker (Hymenoptera: Pteromalidae), *Ecology*, 48: 294–301.

80 Werren, J. H., 1980, 'Sex ratio adaptations to local mate competition in a parasitic wasp', *Science*, 208: 1157–1159.

81 Krombein, K. V., 1967, *Trap Nesting Wasps and Bees—Life Histories, Nests and Associates,* Smithsonian Press: Washington, D.C. Longair, R. W., 1981, 'Sex ratio variations in xylophilous aculeate Hymenoptera', *Evolution*, 35: 597–600.

82 Charnov, E. L., Los-den Hartogh, R. L., Jones, W. T. and van den Assem, J., 1981, 'Sex ratio evolution in a variable environment', *Nature*, 289: 27–33.

83 Clutton-Brock, T., 1982, 'Sons and daughters', *Nature*, 298: 11–13.

84 See, for example, *International Herald Tribune*, 11 November 1982; *The Daily Telegraph*, 2 April 1983; *The Guardian*, 8 April 1983; *Financial Times*, 21 May 1983.

85 Cited by Daly and Wilson (note 73), p. 298.

86 Wilson, M. and Daly, M., 1983, 'Competitiveness, risk-taking and violence: the young male syndrome', in N. A. Chagnon and W. Irons, eds., *Human Sociobiology: New Research and Theory*, forthcoming.

87 Cited by Daly and Wilson (note 73), p. 301.

88 Daly and Wilson (note 15), p. 76.

89 Daly, M. and Wilson, M., 1982, 'Whom are newborn babies said to resemble?', *Ethology and Sociobiology*, 3: 69–78.

90 Murdock, G. P., 1967, *Ethnographic Atlas,* University of Pittsburgh Press: Pittsburgh, Pennsylvania.

91 Faux, S. F., 1981, cited by Daly and Wilson (note 73).

92 Dickemann, M., 1979, quoted by Daly and Wilson (note 73), p. 285.

93 As note 10, p. 17.

94 Beall, C. M., and Goldstein, M. C., 1981, 'Tibetan fraternal polyandry: a test of sociobiological theory', *American Anthropologist*, 83: 5–12.

95 Johnson, R. E., 1970, 'Some correlates of extramarital coitus', *Journal of Marriage and the Family*, 32: 449–456.

96 Sigush, V. and Schmidt, G., 1971, 'Lower-class sexuality: some emotional and social aspects in West German males and females', *Archives of Sexual Behavior*, 1: 29–44.

97 Antonovsky, H. F., 1980, *Adolescent Sexuality: A Study of Attitudes and Behavior,* Lexington Books: Lexington, Massachusetts.

98 Kinsey, A. C., Pomeroy, W. B., Martin, C. E. and Gebhard, P. H., 1953, *Sexual Behavior in the Human Female,* Saunders: Philadelphia, Pennsylvania.

99 Touhey, J. C., 1972, 'Comparison of two dimensions of attitude

similarity on heterosexual attraction', *Journal of Personality and Social Psychology*, 23: 8–10.

100 Low, B. S., 1979, 'Sexual selection and human ornamentation', in N. A. Chagnon and W. Irons, eds., *Evolutionary Biology and Human Social Behavior: An Anthropological Perspective*, Duxbury Press: North Scituate, Massachusetts.

101 Translated and quoted by Daly and Wilson (note 73), p. 293.

102 As note 98.

103 Teismann, M. W., 1975, 'Jealous conflict: a study of verbal interaction and labeling of jealousy among dating couples involved in jealousy improvisations', Doctoral dissertation, University of Connecticut, cited by Daly and Wilson (note 73).

104 Hartung, J., 1981, 'Paternity and inheritance of wealth', *Nature*, 291: 267–268.

105 Greene, P. J., 1978, 'Promiscuity, paternity, and culture', *American Ethnologist*, 5: 151–159.

106 Ashton, G. C., 1980, 'Mismatches in genetic markers in a large family study', *American Journal of Human Genetics*, 32: 601–613.

107 Maynard Smith, J. (note 9), p. 139.

108 Fox, R., 1980, *The Red Lamp of Incest*, Hutchinson: London.

109 Wrangham, R. W., personal communication to J. C.

110 Bell, A. P. and Weinberg, M. S., 1978, *Homosexuality: a Study of Diversity Among Men and Women*, Simon and Schuster: New York.

111 Quoted by Daly, M. and Wilson, M., 1980, 'Male and female', *The Sciences*, March 1980: 22–24. p. 24.

112 Symons, D., 1980, 'Précis of The Evolution of Human Sexuality', *Behavioral and Brain Sciences*, 3: 171–214. p. 181.

113 Symons, D., 1979, *The Evolution of Human Sexuality*, Oxford University Press: Oxford. p. 304.

114 Ralls, K., 1977, 'Sexual dimorphism in mammals: avian models and unanswered questions', *American Naturalist*, 111: 917–938.

115 Alexander, R. D., Hoogland, J. L., Howard, R. D., Noonan, K. M. and Sherman, P. W., 1979, 'Sexual dimorphisms and breeding systems in pinnipeds, ungulates, primates, and humans', in N. A. Chagnon and W. Irons, eds, *Evolutionary Biology and Human Social Behaviour: An Anthropological Perspective*, Duxbury Press: North Scituate, Massachusetts.

116 Cited by Alexander, R. D., *et al.* (note 115).

117 Cited by Alexander, R. D., *et al.* (note 115).

118 As note 58, p. 143.

119 Clutton-Brock, T. H. and Harvey, P. H., 1977, 'Primate ecology and social organization', *Journal of Zoology*, 183: 1–39.

120 Selander, R. K., 1966, 'Sexual dimorphism and differential niche utilization in birds', *Condor,* 68: 113–151.

121 Cline, D. R., Siniff, D. B. and Erickson, A. W., 1971, 'Underwater copulation of the Weddell seal', *Journal of Mammalogy,* 52: 216–218.

122 Berry, J. F. and Shine, R., 1980, 'Sexual size dimorphism and sexual selection in turtles (Order Testudines)', *Oecologia,* 44: 185–191.

123 Harcourt, A. H., Stewart, K., and Fossey, D., 1976, 'Male emigration and female transfer in wild mountain gorilla', *Nature,* 263: 226–227. See also Veit, P. G., 1982, 'Gorilla society', *Natural History,* March 1982: 48–58.

124 Short, R. V., 1981, 'Sexual selection in man and the great apes', in C. E. Graham, ed., *Reproductive Biology of the Great Apes,* Academic Press: New York.

125 Goodall, J., 1983, *In the Shadow of Man,* Houghton Mifflin: Boston.

126 Wrangham, R. W., 'The behavioural ecology of chimpanzees in Gombe National Park, Tanzania', Doctoral Dissertation, Cambridge University.

127 Tutin, C. E. G. and McGinnis, P. R., 1981, 'Chimpanzee reproduction in the wild,' in C. E. Graham, ed., *Reproductive Biology of the Great Apes,* Academic Press: New York.

128 Warner, H., Martin, D. E. and Keeling, M. E., 1974, 'Electroejaculation of the great apes', *Annals of Biomedical Engineering,* 2: 419–432. See also Short, R. V., 1981 (note 124).

129 Cauthery, P., Stanway, A. and Stanway, P., 1983, *The Complete Book of Love & Sex: A Guide for All the Family,* Century Publishing: London.

130 Morris, D., 1967, *The Naked Ape,* McGraw-Hill: New York.

131 Keilman, D. G., 1977, 'Monogamy in mammals', *Quarterly Review of Biology,* 52: 39–69.

132 Alexander, R. D. and Noonan, K. M., 1979, 'Concealment of ovulation, parental care, and human social evolution', in N. A. Chagnon and W. Irons, eds., *Evolutionary Biology and Human Social Behavior: An Anthropological Perspective,* Duxbury Press: North Scituate, Massachusetts. p. 444.

133 Lovejoy, C. O., 1981, 'The origin of man', *Science,* 211: 341–350.

134 Quoted by Johanson, D. C. and Edey, M. A., 1981, *Lucy: The Beginnings of Humankind,* Simon & Schuster: New York. p. 334.

135 As note 134, p. 337.

136 O'Herlihy, C. and Robinson, H. P., 1980, 'Mittelschmerz is a preovulatory phenomenon', *British Medical Journal,* 280: 986.

137 Hill, E. and Wenzl, P., 1981, 'Variation in ornamentation and behavior in a discotheque for females observed at differing menstrual

phases', paper presented to the Animal Behavior Society, Knoxville, Tennessee, cited by Daly and Wilson (note 73).

138 Various authors, 1982, 'Models of human evolution', *Science*, 217: 295–394.

139 As note 133, p. 346.

140 As note 7.

141 Burley, N., 1979, 'The evolution of concealed ovulation', *American Naturalist*, 114: 835–858.

142 Adams, D. B., Gold, A. R. and Burt, A. D., 1978, 'Rise in female-initiated sexual activity at ovulation and its suppression by oral contraceptives', *New England Journal of Medicine*, 229: 1145–1150.

143 Quoted by Wolfe, L. D., *et al.*, 1982 (note 134), p. 302.

144 McLintock, M. K., 1971, 'Menstrual synchrony and suppression', *Nature*, 229: 244–245.

145 As note 132.

146 Eysenck, H. J. and Wilson, G., 1979, *The Psychology of Sex*, J. M. Dent: London, p. 176.

147 As note 146, p. 161.

148 Allen, M. L. and Lemmon, W. B., 1981, 'Orgasm in female primates', *American Journal of Primatology*, 1: 15–34. p. 23.

149 As note 146, p. 174.

150 As note 130.

151 As note 146, p. 180.

152 Vance, E. B. and Wagner, N. N., 1976, 'Written description of orgasm: a study of sex differences', *Archives of Sexual Behaviour*, 5: 87–98.

153 Cited by Alexander and Noonan (note 132), p. 451.

154 Marshall, D. S., 1971, cited by Wilson, G., 1981, *Love and Instinct*, Temple Smith: London. pp. 145–146.

155 Ben Shaul, D. M., 1962, 'The composition of the milk of wild animals', *International Zoo Yearbook*, 4: 333–342.

156 Hamilton, W. D., Henderson, P. A. and Moran, N. A., 1981, 'Fluctuation of environment and coevolved antagonist polymorphism as factors in the maintenance of sex', in Alexander, R. D. and Tinkle, D. W., eds., *Natural Selection and Social Behavior*, Chiron: New York.

157 Levin, D. A., 1975, 'Pest pressure and recombination systems in plants', *American Naturalist*, 109: 437–451. p. 439.

158 As note 157, p. 441.

159 Hamilton, W. D., 1980, 'Sex versus non-sex versus parasite', *Oikos*, 35: 282–290.

160 Hamilton, W. D., 1982, 'Pathogens as causes of genetic diversity in their host populations', in R. M. Anderson and R. M. May, eds.,

Population Biology of Infectious Diseases, Dahlem Konferenzen 1982, Springer-Verlag: Berlin. pp. 270–271.

161 As note 160, pp. 271–272.

162 As note 159, p. 283.

163 As note 159, pp. 289–290.

164 Dausset, J., 1981, 'The major histocompatibility complex in man: past, present and future concepts', *Science*, 213: 1469–1474. p. 1469.

165 As note 164, p. 1473.

166 We cannot go into the techniques of genetic engineering here. For readers who want to understand this new and exciting technology, one of us has written a book about it: Cherfas, J., 1983, *Man-Made Life: An Overview of the Science, Technology, and Commerce of Genetic Engineering*, Pantheon: New York.

167 Robertson, M., 1983, 'Immunity, evolution and self-recognition', *New Scientist*, 98: 198–200.

168 Cited by Jones, J. S. and Partridge, L., 1983, 'Tissue rejection: the price of sexual acceptance?' *Nature*, 304: 484–485.

169 Bremermann, H. J. 1980, 'Sex and polymorphism as strategies in host-pathogen interactions', *Journal of Theoretical Biology*, 87: 671–702.

170 As note 160, p. 290.

171 Toynbee, P. 1983, 'Caught between an old and a new mythology about the nature of men and women', *The Guardian*, 26, September 1983. p. 10.

INDEX

INDEX

ABOUT THE AUTHORS

Dr. Jeremy Cherfas is a writer and broadcaster, and a consultant on *New Scientist*. He has worked on such major series as BBCI's *Zoo 2000*, which was scheduled for broadcast in the autumn of 1984. Dr. John Gribbin, also a consultant on *New Scientist*, is the author of *Spacewarps* and co-author of two novels, *The Sixth Winter* and *Brother Esau*. Jeremy Cherfas and John Gribbin's first collaboration, the highly acclaimed *The Monkey Puzzle*, was published in 1982.